THE HAND THAT HOLDS THE CAMERA

GARLAND REFERENCE LIBRARY
OF THE HUMANITIES (VOL. 688)

THE HAND THAT HOLDS THE CAMERA

Interviews with Women Film
and Video Directors

Lynn Fieldman Miller

GARLAND PUBLISHING, INC.
NEW YORK & LONDON 1988

Library of Congress Cataloging-in-Publication Data

Miller, Lynn F.
The hand that holds the camera : interviews with
women film and video directors / Lynn Fieldman Miller.
      p. cm.—(Garland reference library of the humani-
ties : vol. 688)
      Includes index.
      ISBN 0-8240-8530-2 (alk. paper)
      1. Women motion picture producers and direc-
tors—United States—Interviews.   2. Women television
producers and directors—United States—Interviews.
I. Title. II. Series.
   PN1998.2.M5 1988
   791.43′0233′0922—dc 19   87-32871

Design by Renata Gomes

Printed on acid-free, 250-year-life paper
Manufactured in the United States of America

To the memory of my mother
Helen Fieldman

ACKNOWLEDGMENTS

I am grateful to the Rutgers University Research Council for providing grant funding for tapes, travel money, and secretarial support and to the Rutgers University Faculty Academic Study Program for a one-year sabbatical leave to work on the book in 1985–86. I also thank Susan Capobianco, who transcribed the tapes of the interviews, patiently retyped them, and assisted me as secretary, typist, and general helper on the project. Thanks also to the talented women interviewed here who responded to my many requests for more information.

CONTENTS

INTRODUCTION

In the last twenty years people, whether they are minority group members and/or women, have been made increasingly aware that the images that they see help shape their self-concepts and the society. Even before the onset of image-making technologies, from the printing press to the camera (still and motion) and now television, there were mirrors, stories, and other reflections of the self through the lenses of cultural norms and expectations.[1]

The images of girls and women in books, magazines, ads, films, and on television influence the way that girls and women see themselves. It is therefore important and useful for women to control the images in these powerful media, to ensure that real women's lives and selves are reflected. The "hand that holds the camera" has ruled the images of women shown in the media; now that hand will more often be a woman's hand. Will this make a difference?

Generally, women film directors have had more success with experimental and independently produced feminist documentary films than with Hollywood commercial films, with some notable exceptions; directors like Dorothy Arzner in the 1930s and 1940s and, more recently, the Australian Gillian Armstrong have achieved some measure of finan-

1. Jan Rosenberg in her introduction to her *Women's Reflections: The Feminist Film Movement* (Ann Arbor: UMI Research Press, 1983) provides a useful explanation of the image question.

cial and critical success. Susan Seidleman's *Desperately Seeking Susan* is anther example of a commercial success for a woman director.

But how does the work of an independent woman filmmaker or video artist help women rethink themselves and the society?

Elaine Showalter[2] and other scholars of women's literature have argued that it has made a difference when a woman holds the pen, pounds the typewriter, or processes the words that result in novels, stories, poetry, and other forms of literature. In film and video the technology of production is different but the theory remains the same: there is such a thing as women's culture expressed through the minds and experiences of women. Filmmaking and video production can be thought of as forms of writing; the hieroglyphics are produced not with pen and ink or word processors but with the complex technology of the most collaborative of art forms. It is "writing," as dance is a form of writing with one's body and theater performance is a form of writing with one's total being.

The question for filmmakers and video producers, as it has always been for all artists, is, who gets to call the shots? In Hollywood, the question is, who gets the final cut? This is, of course, a problem for all artists in Hollywood, not just for women directors. Hollywood, in this context, is a shorthand way of saying the large industrial complex that controls the image-making that is released in major mass culture feature films and mainstream television.

2. Elaine Showalter, *A Literature of Their Own* (Princeton, N.J.: Princeton University Press, c1977), pp. 7, 12.

Hollywood has undeniably been a powerful force in American culture. When a woman director goes to Hollywood to "make it" in film, a feminist audience often perceives a compromising of vision that was clearer and more distinctly female, if not feminist, prior to the Hollywoodization of that director. Although Hollywood is a dream factory, its emphasis is on factory. It sells a product. The product must make a profit, and there are tried and true clichés and genres that pull in the dollars. It is not in Hollywood productions or commercial television that you can best see the difference that a woman's hand holding the camera and a woman's eye looking through the viewfinder makes in creating the kinds of images that can reconstruct the world.

In journals as disparate as *Heresies* and *Ms.*, women theorists, critics, and reviewers of film and video have decried the paucity of positive images of women in the mass media. There have been several studies that have demonstrated that the images that one sees of women on the large movie screen and on the small television screen do affect the way generations of women view themselves. The question for feminists is, if there is an incongruence between what they see on the screens and what happens in their lives, what besides not going to the movies or not turning on the television can they do about it?

There are a number of women who have chosen to function independent of Hollywood and commercial television, to produce images that are truer constructions of what women's lives feel like and what women's lives mean to women. Prominent among feminist theorists about film is Laura Mulvey who, in her writing[3] and in her filmmaking, claims that the very apparatus of the filmmaker's art—the viewfinder, the camera—is male, voyeuristic, phallocentric, scopophiliac, invasive of privacy, and that the act of filmmaking is a kind of rape. Brian De Palma's films easily exemplify this theory, for in his films women are the meat for the cinematic grinding apparatus. The object of the gaze, it is contended by some theorists of cinema, is always female and the subject or viewer is presumed to be male. Even Woody Allen's films can be analyzed from this perspective. Hollywood filmmakers usually presume the viewer is a man between the ages of 16 and 29. This can be demonstrated by looking at film after film by obviously misogynist filmmakers from Hitchcock to De Palma and can be applied by analogy to other art forms such as painting and sculpture. Many people thought that the role of the female should only be that of nude model for sculpture or painting. The active element in the· painting was considered to be the male artist who looked at, for inspiration, the usually nude female model, very often his mistress and by extension his muse. By invading her privacy, invading perhaps her boudoir, he painted lyrical (and sometimes not so lyrical) exploitations of her sensuality and her essence as perceived by the male gaze. However, when women were allowed to study painting and to work from life, the experience was different. Painting was transformed. Mary Cassatt painted real mothers with real children in a way that was different from, say, Bellini's idealized Madonna and Child.

3. Laura Mulvey, "Visual Pleasure and the Narrative Cinema," *Screen* 16, No. 3 (Autumn 1975), 6–18.

Introduction

Art history in recent years is replete with studies[4] that show that when women wield the paint brush or the sculptors' tools, even when the subject is a nude female, the result is different because the value system is different. The gaze itself is qualitatively different, even when the woman artist is the lover of the woman model.

The work of the women interviewed here are exemplary cases of how a woman's gaze can be different; one begins with the selection of material. All art is basically selection; even in making purely documentary films, one chooses a subject. These women choose subjects that are paradoxically both small and large. They often deal with the personal dilemmas of an individual woman.

The emphasis on intimacy in the use of the camera is a striking characteristic of much of the work and partially defines it as feminist. The subjects of these women's recent work are both intimate and global; they could apply to women anywhere. Many of the themes derive from life experiences. The women sometimes use work created by others or sometimes write their own scripts based on autobiographical material or the lives of others. But always the choice is to work with personal and intimate thoughts, feelings, and experiences of women in dilemmas that are specific and yet transcend the specific. By investigating the personal, they show that the personal is both political and universal. This selection of personal material often characterizes the best of the work of women film-

4. For example, Linda Nochlin's "Why Have There Been No Great Women Artists?," *Art News* 69, No. 9 (January 1971), 22–39, 67–71.

makers and video artists, whether they are independent filmmakers or filmmakers who produce
feature-length films.

(It is true that men sometimes also select the
personal; for example, Woody Allen's work has the
surface gloss of the personal, but he undercuts
himself and his female subjects by focusing on neu-
rosis, which he derides and manipulates. He is
funny. We like and enjoy some of his films, but we
wonder whether he likes women. Obsesses, yes.
Uses, yes. Likes or understands? One must wonder.)

Another characteristic of these women's work is
the careful choice of talent. Talent is a word used in
film and theater to mean the actor, dancer, performer—the person before the camera's eye. Most
often, these artists do not select idealized women,
like *Vogue* or *Seventeen Magazine* models, but
choose "real" women to work with. They tend to
use women whom one can call original looking.
Many of them are beautiful, but that is not the
point. None of them is perfect and the camera seeks
to explore their flaws and their beauty in the way a
lover explores one's flaws and beauty. Knowing the
flaws makes the beauty even more treasured.

The women that we see in these works are vastly
different from the kind of talent selected by mainstream film- and videomakers. The talent selection
characteristic of feminist film and video practice
deliberately eschews the slick and glamorous in
favor of the gritty and subtle beauty of real women.
By "real" I do not mean merely ordinary. That is
another characteristic of the work of the artists
interviewed. Regardless of the origin of the script,

the stories that these women tell deal with the heroism in women's lives—the heroic decisions and
choices that women make just to live their lives,
day in and day out. By choosing women with a
certain look to perform in their works, the directors
and producers are not saying that these women are
ordinary. They seek the extraordinary in what is
normally regarded as ordinary.

The choice of stories and the choice of talent
combine to demonstrate another element of work
that characterizes feminist practice in film and
video. They do not valorize in their female protago-
nists traditional feats of male heroism (as, for example, the producers of *Aliens* did), such as vio-
lence, war exploits, power plays—masculinized
dramatic situations that are so often the central
stuff of the *Star Wars*, cops and robbers, cowboys
and Indians, car chase fare we are fed in the mass
culture. Most of the people in the works are considered heroic by the women directors. They think
that the choices these women are making are
heroic choices, even if they seem small. How to talk
at all; how to talk to your father; how to talk to your
mother; how to tell about your abortion.

Given the constraints to which women have been
socialized, each character in many of these works
represents a triumph over the inhibitions that lead
to silence, and the most dramatic moments in many
of these works occur when the characters decide to
speak. This breakthrough from silence to speech is
the most dramatic and heroic choice that women
artists themselves make in their lives. Finding one's
voice and using it effectively is a heroic experience
for many women. (See Belenky, Clinchy, Gold-

berger, and Taruli's *Women's Ways of Knowing,* published in 1986, by Basic Books, New York.)

The issue of speaking in one's own voice goes back in filmmaking history to Dorothy Arzner in the 1930s, one of the first women Hollywood directors. In her film, *Dance, Girl, Dance* Arzner depicts the breakthrough when the silent ballet dancer Judy, played by Maureen O'Hara, confronts the male audience and speaks. She tells them that their gaze demeans her, that their laughter harms her, and that she doesn't want to be seen merely as an object of the male gaze any longer.

Demonstrating the heroic nature of the act of female speech itself is characteristic of feminist film and video practice. It is an assertion that a woman can find her own voice and her own language, and use them to state the truth about her condition and her life.

The women interviewed here have become the heroes of their own lives, after making a series of difficult choices and learning to speak the language of film and video.

A central element in many, but by no means all, feminist films and videos is intimacy. In much of the work of these directors, the women to whom we are listening open themselves up to us, revealing strengths and weaknesses, a multitude of doubts and hopes and fears. They seem to trust us not to judge them harshly or to laugh at them or to draw away from them, but to empathize with their confidences the way we would with a friend, a neighbor, a relative, or perhaps a client. The intimate portrait, whether in documentary or fiction film, is characteristic of feminist practice in film and video. Asking a woman to consider the camera as a friend and a confidante, that is, as an ally, rather than as a rapist or voyeur, allows her to trust the filmmaker, to trust the video producer, and by extension to trust the audience not to invade her with their gaze, to rape her with their gaze, but to understand and respect her, to see her as she wishes to be seen—a valid, complex, adult, fully human being.

The women interviewed here have journeyed through many art forms, from architecture, dance, painting, and sculpture to film and video. These personal journeys represented a quest for a personal aesthetic that incorporates a personal ethic, a personal way of dealing with other human beings. The blending of aesthetic with ethic and the deliberate search for a personal aesthetic-ethic are also hallmarks of feminist film and video practice. Rather than succumb to the ready-made, ready-to-wear aesthetics dictated by Hollywood genres or mainstream television, rather than succumb to ethics that are prescribed by a society's mores or parental dicta, these women have searched through their whole lives to come to a personal vision of what is good and true and beautiful. They blend both the search and the vision in their work. Feminist filmmakers, such as Michelle Citron and Amalie Rothschild, and video artists, like Doris Chase and Tami Gold, who seek to blend an esthetic and an ethic with a personal vision, demonstrate this particularly feminist way of making films.

Some filmmakers, some critics, and even some feminist scholars have argued that it doesn't make a difference that a woman is the artist, whatever the medium, and that to argue that women's work in the arts is different from men's work is essentialist, denigrating, and "ghettoizing." I do not agree. I do not know if the evidence supports the existence of women's imagery or a particular female iconography or a specifically female approach to filmmaking that is not accessible to men. I would be enchanted to learn that men could indeed learn what I here call feminist practices and apply them to their work. One thing I do know is that there is such a thing in this culture as a woman's life as it is lived in a woman's body even though not all women have the same experiences in their lives or in their bodies. (For example, not all women who choose to become mothers can become biological mothers.) But there is a woman's culture, through choice or default, and women artists, including women filmmakers and video producers, do have identifiable methods, approaches, visions. Furthermore, I am convinced a reading of a woman's life and of that woman's work will reveal practices that are definably feminist.

Lynn F. Miller
Highland Park, N.J.
May 1987

DORIS TOTTEN CHASE

2   Doris Totten Chase

Doris Chase is a major innovator in the use of video as art, having invented new genres of video sculpture, dance, and drama. A native of Seattle, Chase studied architecture at the University of Washington, worked as a painter for fifteen years, then as a sculptor for a decade. She had her first New York show in 1962. Her work is shown in festivals in Berlin, London, Paris, Los Angeles, and New York.

Born in Seattle, Washington, on April 29, 1923, to Helen Feeney and William Totten, Doris Chase attended the University of Washington between 1941 and 1942. She holds an honorary Ph.D. from the University of Colorado, awarded in 1974. She has two sons, Gregary Totten Chase and Rantall Totten Chase. Her work has been exhibited in many one-woman shows, including The Formes Gallery, Tokyo, Japan, 1970; the Portland, Oregon, Art Museum, 1976 and 1980; the Museum of Modern Art, New York City, 1978 and 1980; The Hirschorn Museum, Washington, D.C., 1974 and 1977. She is a frequent guest lecturer and speaker, having given presentations at such institutions as Harvard University; SUNY Purchase; UCLA; Brooklyn College; Fordham University, Sarah Lawrence College; University of Michigan; Hunter College; University of Washington; British Film Institute; Academy of Film, Prague; National Museum of Romania, Bucarest; Melbourne University, Australia; Museum of Fine Art in San Paulo, Brazil, and The New School, New York City.

Chase is a member of Women Artist Filmmakers, the New York Film Council, and the Association of Independent Video and Film Producers. She resides in New York City, at the Chelsea Hotel.

Doris Totten Chase 3

Chase's films and videos are in the permanent collection of the Lincoln Center Performing Arts Library, New York City; Centre Pompidou, Paris; Museum of Modern Art, New York City; etc.

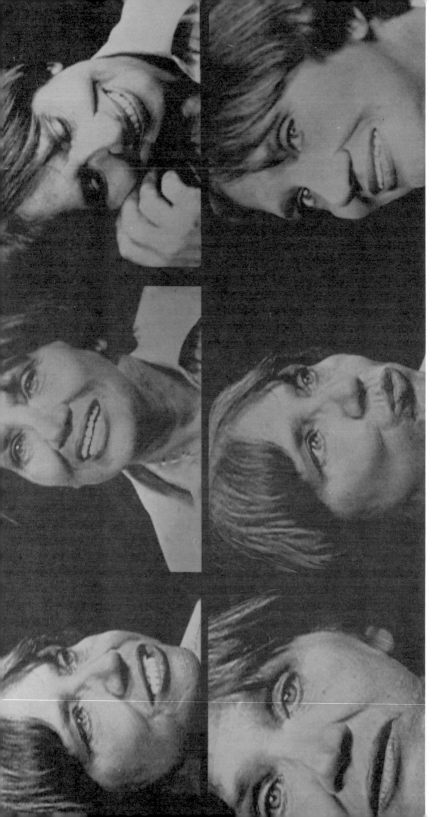

Jennie Ventriss in *Glass Curtain*. Doris Chase *Concepts*.

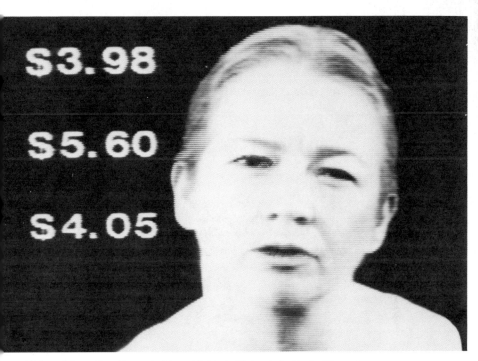

Mabou Mines: Lee Breuer's *Lies* with Ruth Maleczech. Doris Chase *Concepts.*

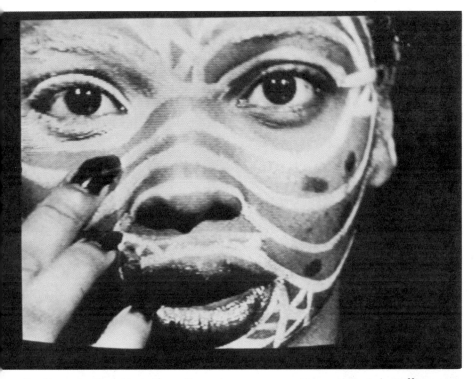

Pat Patton in *Mask.* Doris Chase *Concepts.*   Photo credit: Judy Hoffman.

INTERVIEW

Lynn Miller's Interview with Doris Chase on April 10, 1985.

[Lynn Miller] L) Tell me about making the transition from painting and sculpture, the so-called traditional [artistic] media, into film and video. You mentioned that you wanted to capture the excitement of a live performance and also to control it more, to control the form and color. . . . You were just saying that you think it is important for your work on women to . . .

[Doris Chase] D) . . . be seen, and the only way to be seen is to have something published about it.

L) Why do you think it is so important?

D) That which is not written about does not exist. You see—I don't have a distributor, an agent, a public relations person. I've completed 30 films and another 30 videotapes. One way to help them become visible is by welcoming someone like you, who will write an exciting article and then more people will want to view the tapes. They'll discover a magic and see how brilliant are some of these women, who write, who compose, and who perform superbly.

L) Is the sense of urgency that you feel personal or do you think that there is something in the times that makes it so?

D) For me, it's doubly urgent. First, I don't know how much longer I will have the energy to continue producing and directing on miniscule

5

budgets. The second urgency is because in many fields, instead of gaining placement, women are losing, are slipping back to conditions similar to those of pre-1970.

L) Is that true in independent video and film too?

D) In video it is not quite as apparent because video is such a new field. Women in video are almost equal in exhibitions and shows that are given. However, you will find examples of sexism. Visual Studies in Rochester recently had a show and they advertised it as a comprehensive view of video and not one woman was included.

L) Not one? That's a joke. Who chose the show at Visual Studies at Rochester?

D) The director of the Boston Museum of Contemporary Art, David Ross, curated the show. There is an urgency in the universities and colleges also. Many times I speak to women who are in the departments, theater departments, film departments, and they have similar problems. Not many of them are tenured, and not many are professors.

L) That's precisely right.

D) The people who program exhibitions, the people who write the curriculum, the people who choose what will be seen and who will be teaching are still either men or . . . so brainwashed by the system that they're almost more male oriented than the men who are in charge.

L) What about the journals that have articles about video?

D) There aren't too many written about video art. Some of the art magazines are starting to recognize it as an art form. *Videography* was one of the few, but it is becoming more and more technically oriented.

L) What about the galleries, the video distributors? There are a few.

D) Howard Wise of Electronic Arts Intermix is a distributor. I have not seen his catalog recently, but I think one might find that it is about 15 to 20% women. The Kitchen has a lot of performance artists' tapes and some video art. Global Village is very open to women. One thing that is very depressing is to look in the film study collections of Anthology Film Archives or of the Museum of Modern Art or to look at the Museum of Modern Art's circulating film collection.

L) And then do they say that it is an aesthetic judgment, that women do not make great art?

D) Well, they're barely recognized. Little is written about women. Maya Deren, dead for 20 years, is now being recognized.

L) It's the same thing with the other arts. When I was doing women artists' shows at Douglass it was the same kind of thing. "Well, there are no great women artists." But then, of course, the ones we know of through the Brooklyn Museum's show of artists from the 1550s to 1950s were there, ignored over the centuries. History has ignored them, so how can you know if they are great or not? Then there is the question of who's doing the assessment of greatness, of what is aesthetically valid.

D) Or who's showing it . . .

L) . . . and it's usually men . . .

D) Yes, men are showing it. Who is curating the shows? Who is writing the catalogs?

L) But are we buying it? I keep asking if perhaps we may be sacrificing formal standards in favor of our political beliefs. What about the political thing? I get worried about the infiltration of aesthetics by politics. Is that an issue, or not?

D) Until this time in my life I have not taken a political stand in my art. I felt that art, like religion, need not be politically involved. Painting is an abstract. Sculpture is an abstract. Music is an abstract.

L) Allegedly it does not matter if it is made by a man or a woman.

D) Except that for many years I painted under the signature of D. Chase. And I know many women who were in exactly the same situation. The minute one saw a name like Betty or Jean or Marian the art was placed in a different category.

L) And nobody buys it.

D) Galleries will still not show women to the same degree as men because the public will not invest in them. Women are not a viable commodity.

L) That's not true in film and video?

D) That's a difficult question. Very few "films as art" are purchased.

L) We buy, but I find that the women who are

the most powerful are the documentarists. Certain people have made it in film and video documentary. Women are doing well in that field.

D) Basically I am speaking about "film as art," or "video art." It's the same in theater, in music. How many women composers have you ever heard or read about?

L) And it isn't because there aren't any.

D) There are many very fine women composers and there are a lot of fine playwrights. There are innumerable fine directors and producers. But we don't often read about them or hear about them.

L) They're invisible.

D) They don't exist unless something is written about them. That is why I think that what you are doing is very important. Furthermore, if you could introduce some of the students at Rutgers to women artists and encourage them to write about them, there are many who could participate.

L) Mostly women students.

D) The ones who are writing a thesis or dissertation.

L) In the arts there is a huge number of women students.

D) They could research and write theses about creative women. This is an area where our strength could develop.

L) What about your personal experiences in terms of being a woman artist, a woman filmmaker, and a woman video artist, encountering sexism? Did that ever happen? Were you turned away or excluded?

D) I think that many of us are turned away. If there is an anthology or a collection being made we are often not purchased. If one looks at the amount of work being done, by both men and women, and then looks at the ratio, the percentages are not in balance. Some of the most imaginative, sensitive work is being done by women.

L) I certainly think so too. The Barnard festival is one wonderful thing, and they have to be commended for that. But it is not enough. . . .

D) If you attend Barnard, you discover that they don't have a film department. The students go to Columbia University, and Columbia film school has one woman on the faculty part-time. She teaches on a Tuesday. I have been collecting information from the various schools for years and continued the depressing research around the country on my lecture presentations at various universities. It is just as bad in the women's colleges. There are reasons for my turning gradually, but very determinedly, to a political stance and to a wish to make a change.

L) They don't have the curriculum, they don't have the faculty, and they don't have the facilities.

D) In many colleges they've created areas called "women's studies"; some are now phasing down for lack of funding. Sadly the women's studies departments can't put energy into seeing that other departments get more women hired. They are having a difficult time staying alive. And they certainly don't have budgets to bring in films or video.

L) I don't know if that is true everywhere. That isn't exactly what is happening at Rutgers, where women's studies is growing, or it seems to be, and, I will knock on wood, is strong and is hanging in there. They have good leadership.

D) I think all of them have good leadership. It's a matter of money and priorities.

L) Do you teach, by the way?

D) No longer; I do occasional workshops and lecturing. As a guest lecturer I make it a point to talk to the faculty about the ratio of male to female teachers, the ratio of professorships, and tenure. Disappointingly it is less now than in 1972.

L) We have lost ground over the last decade. And it also doesn't make you popular: I am sure they don't like to hear it raised.

D) And they don't like to give this information. I made six phone calls before someone would finally send me the list of the faculty at Columbia University Film School. After I read it I could understand why.

L) It makes them uncomfortable. What about N.Y.U.?

D) Not much better.

L) I am beginning to feel very lucky to be at Rutgers; it seems like a hotbed of feminism compared to the other places.

D) In the top ten or twenty colleges, women don't have much of a chance.

L) Like Yale and . . .

D) Columbia, Harvard, Dartmouth, Cornell.

L) Well, Princeton was taking chances on visiting artists during the 1970s. Sam Hunter was the chair of the visual arts department and he was bringing in people like Joan Snyder. Maybe not taking chances in video, although he did bring in some video artists. He brought in Gloria Deitscher from D Visions. I think it was 1979 or 1980, so it is possible to teach at Princeton. I don't know how one goes about it.

Doris, it sounds to me from your talk that you are a feminist simply because you perceive inequities.

D) I had not been working as a feminist until the last two or three years. The new theater pieces opened a Pandora's Box. When you view *Electra Tries to Speak* you hear yourself. Some of the tapes are consciousness-raising.

L) We need it again, don't we? The consciousness has sunk rather low.

D) *Glass Curtain* opens the area of the close bonding between mother and daughter, the love and hate, the extreme oneness of the experience of being a daughter and/or mother, and the confrontation that eventual illness and senility bring.

L) *Glass Curtain:* just the very title is paradoxical and suggests seeing through, having access to,

and yet shutting out, saying this is open/closed, the interplay.
Do you have children?

D) I have two sons. One lives in Seattle, the other in Australia. They are both married. My mother is ill now. She is 80 years old and has Alzheimer's disease, which is dreadful. *Glass Curtain* is about this problem and about our relationship. It is the first script I've written and produced. It is the first time I have made any of my writings public.

L) The work is getting more personal.

D) Yes, the production I just finished is *Mask*. It was written by Bonnie Greer, the actress is Pat Patten, and the composer is Craig Gordon. It concerns some of the unique problems in being a black woman. Another in the *Concept* series is *Travels in the Combat Zone*. It was written by Jessica Hagadorn, a fine young Philippine poet who has her own punk-rock band. Her poetry is extremely poignant and strong. The performers are Mary Lum, who is Chinese, and Marilyn Amaral, a black actress. It explores a number of universal problems of women.

L) Tell me about the role of the director in film and video. You are the director.

D) The *Concept* series is a group of theater pieces that have been performed either in off-Broadway situations or as public readings.

L) And are you the director of the performance as well?

D) Not of the theater piece. The only time I

was involved with theater was when I designed and produced the sculpture for a dance work and when my film was used in multimedia performances. I produce film as art and video art. I worked with Pat Birch, Mary Staton, Kei Takei, Jonathan Hollander, and others at various times and that's entirely different.

L) Tell me about that difference.

D) I take a theater piece that is perhaps 2 or 2 and a half hours long and shape sections of it for a total of 30 minutes. It involves the writers and performers. It takes a lot of development. For rehearsals I have an old black-and-white camera and a half-inch reel-to-reel deck. In my apartment I take the table out of the dining area and it becomes a rehearsal stage. I set up a couple of lights, put the camera on a tripod, and we rehearse. I tape, then the actor and I review and discuss it.

L) Instant feedback.

D) Work, rehearse, view. I'm able to visually translate what I can't verbalize. I can show them.

L) It becomes almost a diagnostic tool.

D) It is collaborative, but I can shape the piece.

L) And then what do you do? After you have collaborated, there is a phase where you shape it alone, I assume.

D) I develop the total choreography of movement for the camera and the performance. It is not theater. It is video. I select the intimate movements and gestures of the hands and the face which are most effective. Women's gestures often involve feelings and are very translatable when framed correctly.

L) The Balinese dance, isn't that very gestural? Hands are central.

D) Unlike theater, broad gestures don't work well for my style of video. I coach the performers to do the tight, meaningful, intimate things, so that when I am in production, the camera can go very close, even into the eye. I prefer contained tight gestures. Perhaps this is a feminist approach and I haven't recognized it before. I work in what is described as "portrait space."

L) The imagery that I noticed in your sculpture is the circle—your use of the circle—centrist imagery. That is supposed to be a female symbol. Was that a conscious choice?

D) I think the circle is endemic to all my work. It starts in one place and returns to that place. You experience the totality of it. It may not cover the world. It may not be the extreme universal statement, but it makes a rather compact statement coming full circle.

L) I am very interested in something that you said before—that there are typical female gestures that you think can almost be translated into dance movements.

D) When I program certain gestures of the hands, that is intimate choreography. These are not the broad gestures with the body and feet as in dance. The choreography I am talking about is the relationship between the face and hands.

16   Doris Totten Chase

When I go into a studio I can afford only one day, so everything must be exact and precise. Once we have "set" the movements the performer knows what is going to happen and where. I have the complete storyboard with every phrase that is to be said and every placement of the body at that phrase. When I speak to my camera people, I have shown them: "This is the shot." If I want my camera to pick up the fourth finger and the thumb and two inches of paper, that is on the diagram and they have seen it. I work with three cameras and direct from the control room. I have a crew of ten to fifteen people working, and the camera persons must know the shots I want. The only way I can reinforce that is for them to see it on the storyboard.

L) So you have done all this planning in advance?

D) After four to six months of planning, it is really organizational. The role of director is management, creative in the visual arts sense, but also in social and political techniques.

L) You have to manage people, not just the actors, but the technicians.

D) When I go into the production studio, I don't have to speak to my acting talent because we have worked together a long time. They know what is necessary; they are professionals. They know that when the floor director says "go," they are to start, and we proceed all the way to finish. I do three complete takes.

L) And they have to trust you, and you have to trust them.

D) Precisely, I don't even think of the talent because I have ten or twelve other people to direct. I must talk constantly to my technical director and to my assistant, the three camera people, and the floor director. I have to speak to the audio engineer and the lighting director, watch the makeup and costumes.

L) It's complex. In order to direct those technical elements, do you yourself have to have a complete understanding of the machinery, and what it can do?

D) I know what the machinery can do, and I know what it cannot do, and I expect the best. I don't always get it. Cameras and equipment can break down, or one can get stuck with a careless crew member. During the last couple of productions, I had an audio person who was listening to the radio during taping. It was a disaster. I can't afford expensive production studios so I put up with things that aren't always the greatest.

L) How do you get access to a studio?

D) I usually make a trade, barter showings of my series for production space. Last year I was given three days for three productions. This was in contractual trade for showings of the complete series in March and April on WNYC-TV.

L) This is interesting because this ties back to who controls what gets done and what's talked about, who controls what gets made in the first place. Now with whom do you mostly deal when you try to get access to the studio?

D) After about 52 phone calls, I am usually

able to set up a meeting with someone who is in charge.

L) But I was thinking of who is in charge. Are they mostly women, are they mostly men?

D) I would say men. Most human beings would not put up with these difficulties.

L) It takes energy.

D) And time and patience. I have thick callouses. I don't want to describe how awful it can be sometimes. However, nobody asked me to do this work. Now I want it written about (not necessarily the garbage I have been through). I want the series reviewed for many reasons.

L) Have you ever had a retrospective showing of all your work?

D) That would be something. There have been showings in numerous museums, universities, and festivals, but a full retrospective would take a week. I don't think there would be much of an audience, because you see I really don't have a big name. I am a woman. In fact, I don't know any woman director/producer/filmmaker who would get a large audience.

L) But these are the kinds of things that have to be done. We have to work on them, and it almost doesn't matter if a lot of people come or not. The thing is to do it.

D) It would be great and perhaps some sort of catalog would be written. In five years people might say, "This is important."

L) Exactly, that is what happens. When we started the Women Artists series at Douglass, people said, "Well, why is she doing that, she is nobody, she doesn't know anything." I am not there any more and the series has survived me. It is still going on and major people have shown there and not so major people—and people who had no reputations before—but they're in there; it does work. You have to create your own institutions, as it were.

D) This is the battle, trying to make things happen. I have nine tapes in the *Concept* series, each 28 minutes in length. These are separate from my 12-part dance series, which is doing very well.

L) Are there women in video who control their own studio space, who have their own facilities?

D) A lot of women have their own equipment.

L) No, I mean the studio facilities that you just described that you have to barter so hard to get.

D) If I were to work for a studio or TV station I couldn't do my own work. I'd be working on other people's projects.

L) In terms of the money, the business side of being an artist in any medium, did you just discover that by living and working? Did you go to art school? Did they ever talk about business? About how to earn a living? How to get the money to do your work? A few schools are starting to do this.

D) (Laugh) Do they do it now?

L) . . . or did you perhaps need more of that kind of education?

20 Doris Totten Chase

D) It's absurd that schools don't have as requisites for artists courses dealing with bookkeeping, typing, creative writing, and public relations. All of these are terribly important to an artist. I have always found it difficult to write about my work; it isn't considered nice for a woman to talk about herself. It has taken a long, long time for me to realize that it is all right, really necessary.

L) Well, what about art school? You did go to art school?

D) I studied architecture for two years and took a couple of painting classes.

L) What made you want to be an artist?

D) I was always interested in drawing, painting, and building. There was no question but that I had to create. When I went to university art wasn't considered a sensible course of study. It was suggested I be a teacher. I chose architecture.

L) Everyone suggests that women be teachers.

D) I did teach for a while. I was married at 20 during World War II. After the war was over, we had a son, Gary, and I was ill during his first year. Then we started to build a house. I designed it. It was to be grand, with a beautiful view. While we were building the house, I became pregnant with Randy. Gary was 3 and suddenly my husband contracted polio and was completely paralyzed. So at age 27, it was as if I had three children, as if my life was over—smothered with responsibility. I taught for the next ten years part-time.

L) Was he completely disabled?

D) He could breathe. At the end of six months he was brought home from the hospital in a wheelchair. He learned to use crutches and then later two canes and full leg braces.

L) He was rehabilitated?

D) To a degree, yes. He went back to school and studied accounting.

L) Were you an artist at this time, too?

D) Yes. Without my painting I don't think I could have survived. The work was pretty uneven, but it was there. It kept me alive. That's a heavy one, isn't it? I haven't thought about it for a long time.

L) It's important because I think those intense things do serve us; we use them in some way to energize us.

D) I finally got a divorce.

L) You were in your mid-40s.

D) It was my late forties. By that time I was unconsciously trying to commit suicide. I was getting a worse case of pneumonia each year. I was aiming my car, rather than driving it. It was a case of self-destruction—deep depression and loneliness. It was literally a time in my life when I had to make a decision: was I going to stay and die or was I going to leave and live.

L) So you came to New York. . . .

D) I came to New York and moved into the

Chelsea Hotel. It was as if I had another chance at life.

L) You left your kids, too?

D) I left my kids. One was 20, traveling in Europe, and the other was 24, getting his master's degree at Harvard.

L) So they didn't need you to be there. You probably wouldn't have done it before, when they were younger.

D) I couldn't have left earlier. Too many problems. Too many worries. I just couldn't leave. I wanted to, but I couldn't. I felt responsible to and for everyone. I don't know of any man who would stay with a crippled wife and two small children, when he was 27 years old. He might stay for a year and a half, maybe two, then leave. "Look, I'm a man, I have needs." Society would understand. "Well, of course he couldn't stay, she's a cripple."

L) Or if he stayed, then you assume there is somebody else on the side.

D) Or, "My God, isn't he wonderful to stay, isn't he something more special than anything you can imagine." Usually women will stay, and work, and slave, really much beyond the bearable, and still feel guilty if they leave.

L) Did you read Adrienne Rich's book *Of Woman Born*? You are interested in mothers and children; you should read it. She has a section in which she states that the essential fact about a woman is her "thereness"; you are supposed to be there.

D) Of course, for someone else. It is difficult to be there for oneself; it's trained out of women from the beginning.

L) When we come to discover it late, in our 40s and we suddenly realize it's okay . . .

D) . . . it's okay to be me. It's taken a long time. It's also very okay for me to ask for help to get this series distributed. I want to get it to a large audience and I want to produce more pieces while I still have the energy.

L) Let me ask you about that business of energy, guilt, and timing in one's life and identity: would you have found your own way when the kids were little as you apparently have since you were in your late 40s and on your own? In other words, could you have said, "I want to transform my life by living by myself and going to New York" if your children had been 10 and 14 instead of 20 and 24?

D) Physically and financially, I could not raise two sons alone and I could not desert them. I didn't think I had the strength to give them the discipline, care, and balance as a single woman.

L) Even though you were basically sustaining the whole group.

D) I didn't know that.

L) Physically you made monumental sculptures; physically you lug around camera equipment.

D) I did not think I could do it. We were completely broke. He was in the hospital for six months. We didn't lose the house because there was a polio foundation that stepped in. Insurance went quickly. I had no way of making a living. I could sell stockings in a department store or teach painting. Neither one pays well. I could not possibly manage financially.

L) What was it that gave you the courage, or the hint, or whatever it took to finally leave after 27 years of marriage?

D) As I mentioned before, it was as if I were trying to commit suicide, without admitting it. I was getting increasingly sick each year, spending more time in the hospital.

L) Your body was telling you you wanted out.

D) Yes, plus the fact that after two accidents I still got back in the car and aimed it. I knew I was trying to run away. One of the accidents could have killed several people. I started thinking a bit harder. After doing a lecture in Florida I was heading back to Seattle, and stopped in New York to take time to think, to make a decision as to whether I was going to leave or not. I determined to leave: it was one of those momentous times and it worked. I was able to make a new, exciting life, enjoy another world, and do some very good work.

L) When did you start verging into film? Was it with a sudden break that you left painting and sculpture?

D) I started making films in Seattle in 1969. First the computer film *Circles I* and then *Circles II*, which has the large circular sculpture forms for dance and was done in collaboration with the Mary Staton Dance Ensemble.

L) There was a gradual transformation of your work into film and then into video. Where did you learn to make films and video? You didn't go to school for it obviously. You just taught yourself?

D) I started doing it by watching others.

L) Where did you get the stuff, the equipment?

D) Borrowing, buying second-hand equipment.

L) Do you remember what it was that made you want to start making films?

D) Yes, precisely. I became interested in multi-media and wanted to make a computer film. Also I was doing a lovely theater piece with the circle sculptures and realized I could have an auditorium full of people looking at it more often by putting it on film. I talked to a film company in Seattle and they were interested. They contracted to produce and direct and I said that they could use my sculpture in the film if in turn they would give me the "outs" from the film when they were finished. It was with the "outs" from their film that I made the prize-winning *Circles II.*

L) That's a wonderful story, but that impulse that you are describing sounds almost like a documentary impulse, an impulse to archivally preserve rather than an integral interest in the medium as visual art.

D) In Seattle I had seen a film by Bob Brown and Frank Olvey who had done some gorgeous things with an optical printing process. I knew that

that was precisely what I wanted to do with *Circles*, not a documentation but a kaleidoscope in color separation. I wanted the different areas and movements to be clear and precise. So I collaborated with them on *Circles II* and at the same time we were developing the computer film *Circles I*. When I moved to New York in 1972, video equipment was beginning to be reasonably accessible. I started on the ground floor and have been working with video ever since.

L) Carla Zackson was telling me about you and your mentoring younger women and creating networks between yourself and younger women, encouraging them in their careers because, as she was saying, there are so few role models. Would you talk a little bit about how you do that? About how you feel about that?

D) People write or call and say they would like to work with me. I love to work with young women if they're bright, if they have dreams and good energy. Working here is hard.

L) It takes physical energy as well as emotional energy. . . .

D) They must be able to write well and learn quickly because they get the equivalent of five years' experience in a very short time. It's like a trade school. They learn how to run a camera, a deck (½″ deck as well as ¾″ deck); they work in audio and video editing sessions; they learn to log tapes quickly and precisely. The people who come in here have a lot going for them. I cannot spend time working with low talent people. We have a good exchange; it's as if we are family. When they leave they often get challenging jobs in the media field and then I start training again.

L) They come out of college not really ready to work. . . .

D) They come from a university with a master's degree, or they may still be in school. Often the colleges don't give the young people information about what it's like in the real world. There are many things one must learn fast if one is "going to make it," not necessarily money, but make it as far as a contribution to the world.

L) Do you feel a commitment to provide this experience?

D) I don't put it like that. They come in to learn and I share with them. I particularly wish to act as a mentor for young women, who will someday go out in the world and help other women.

L) Do you recruit them? Or do they find out about you and come to you?

D) They find their way here. Somebody recommends that they talk to me or they send me a letter.

L) You are looking for women specifically? You find that they are different? Or do you want men and women?

D) I am looking for young women because I like to see them get a head start. It's hard for a young person to find work with a professional who can show them the full gamut of possibilities. It is not a commercial or bureaucratic situation in my studio. This is very low key.

L) But they learn. They go with you to some of these bartering situations that you were describing when you are trying to negotiate yourself into a studio. They see the reality of that.

D) They see the reality. They also go in when a contract is negotiated.

L) So you are finishing their education. All that stuff that you said they don't teach in art school, you're providing that absent curriculum.

D) I think young men are more apt to get into these situations while women are often left on the side, looking through the window. It is a help for them to realize that one must know something about law, bookkeeping, and budgets.

L) Just in order to recognize when you are being taken advantage of.

D) As an example—to be able to say, "Let me talk to you about it tomorrow. . . ." In other words, give me grace time. When I was doing the very large sculpture, the steel pieces, the monumental pieces, I was also involved with sculpture for children. I did not realize that one needs to have a manufacturer and a distributor. I thought that if I designed the pieces, made the molds, produced them, and got them into research centers, they would take off magically. I was naive not to realize that business is business, and if you don't have distribution, publicity, marketing plans, and money behind a new concept, nothing happens.

L) Is that true in film and video also?

D) Yes.

L) How many young women interns have you had over the years?

D) (Laugh) I don't know. I have no idea.

L) Do any of them get discouraged? Do they mostly get encouraged and supported? Seeing how tough it is, I mean?

D) I don't know.

L) Have any of them gone on to exciting careers? You say they go into media. Have you noticed their work? Have you followed it?

D) A couple of them are television editors. One is at ABC and one is at CBS, and that is very tough, high pressure. One of them works for six months so she can travel for six months. Another is in Paris with her own production and distribution company.

L) You stay in touch with them?

D) Oh, yes.

L) Something else I wanted to ask you about: I noticed in the writing about your work and just seeing the imagery a suggestion of goddess imagery.

D) The next script I want to write concerns women's spirituality. For the past several years I have been extremely interested in the boundaries within which women are held by all religions. Religions keep woman in her place. For instance, if you look at the Bible, it's restrictive and completely patristic. Beginning with Adam's rib, we never had a chance. Elaine Pagels, author of the book *The*

Gnostic Gospels, is researching and writing in an extremely scholarly and exciting fashion. Among the interesting facts is [that there was] a Gospel of Mary and that there were women Apostles. Mary was one of the Apostles (and Jesus' favorite). This is the same Mary Magdalene whom most of us have heard described as a harlot and fallen woman. The documents found at NAG Hamadi were Coptic translations from the Greek and date from 120 to 300 AD. They were discovered hidden in Egypt in 1945. What evidently happened is that the early ruling powers of Christianity decided they could not accept certain ideas and still maintain their strengths. So they discarded a great deal of information about God and women and created this biased patriarchal Bible. Judaism led the way for Christianity. Most religions are similar. Women should be owned, face and body, stay on the balcony, walk behind, not give the sacrament, keep their place, serve men. . . . This is one large stone that we all have to recognize and deal with. It is written.

L) Yes, and how can you be religious and worship that God? . . . I cannot. But I do have religious impulses.

D) I have a great spiritual hunger and need, a strong religious impulse. Recent publications like *Gnostic Gospels* have been such a relief and release to me, to realize that before men had written the Bible, there were goddesses and apostles and mystics and witches and they were helpful and they were nurturing. One suggestion that Pagels offers is that God was androgynous. Mother God was the spiritual; father God was the physical. They were one.

L) Well, the "party" line is that God has no sex and no body, in Judaism certainly.

D) But *He* says . . .

L) Right, right, . . . and it's the *Lord.*

D) *He,* the Lord, God, the father, God, the son. They're all men.

L) What about in your own work, though? How does religion get in?

D) In "Mask," I insisted on including a speech about the mother God. In the context of the rest of it, it works. In "Glass Curtain" I put in "God the mother/God the father" as part of the script. I am trying to add spiritual thoughts into the projects little by little. I've been given a fellowship at the MacDowell Colony to work on a script based on the religious dilemmas of women. I have no idea how I am going to approach it.

L) Talk into a tape.

D) That will be the beginning. "In the beginning there was the tape and then there was the pencil."

The other script I want to write concerns women's work. What is women's work? Could it be painting, or sculpture, or writing?

L) No, that's not work. Art isn't work.

D) That's right, that's pleasure. If a man does it, then it's his work, his creative process. But women's work, if one is a writer, what's the work? Work is to make beds, do dishes, cook, clean house. But the little play, the little creative work for a woman, what is it? A hobby? I don't know how I'm going to approach these subjects, but I am going to give them a try.

L) That business of play, by the way, is something I observed when I was watching all your tapes. As serious and committed and hard-working as you evidently are, there is always that spirit of playfulness, of playing with the medium, whatever the medium is. I think certainly this is true with the technology of video—that you are at play, and I don't see that as a denigrating description. I see that as a term of praise because you do explore more when you are willing to play—and I certainly saw that in the dance piece shown at the Barnard Film Festival—yet it is all controlled play.

D) The play is in the imagining and dreaming. The minute I am working with the tools of technology, the play is over; if I had easy access it would be different. Time is very limited and precious. For the piece *Jazz Dance* that you saw at Barnard, I had 60 minutes to totally change the timing and pacing. In other words, a complete choreographic revamping. When I am in the production or editing studio it is not play. People say it looks like improvising, but it is very studied and well-planned improvisation. I have completed *Table for One*, starring Geraldine Page. I think of this as a pilot for a new series involving mature dramatic artists, using leading American actresses. I want to create a new image for television of the woman who is fifty years or older. Wish me luck. It is not an easy project to launch. It should be exciting. In our youth-oriented society maturing adults and those of middle age are not adequately portrayed in the media. It is my intention to bring to the viewer's mind a more complete picture of the single woman as a dynamic, integral part of our society, to draw from a wide range of subjects including the difficulties of loneliness and of growing old gracefully, and to give a fresh view of today's mature woman.

Post Script: Chase's *Table for One* was the prototype for the *By Herself* series, hosted by Jane Fonda, a six-part dramatic series for television. The *By Herself* series denotes Chase as executive producer and director.

CHRONOLOGY

A Dancer (with Luise Rainer)	1987
Dear Papa (with Anne Jackson)	1986
Table for One (with Geraldine Page)	1985
Doris Chase: Portrait of an Artist	1985
An Introduction to Video and Sculpture: Thirty Second Clips	1984
Plexi Radar Gate	1983
Glass Curtain	1983
Three Story Suite	1983
Mask	1983
Electra Tries to Speak	1982
Travels in the Combat Zone	1982
Conversation	1981
Skyfish	1981
Moon Defined	1980
Third Movement	1980
Window	1980
Lies	1980
Gay Delanghe	1979

Cube Defined	1979
Jazz Dance	1979
Circling	1979
Nashville Dance	1979
Sara Rudner	1978
Variation Two	1978
Dance Outline	1978
Dance Frame	1978
Jonathan and the Rocker	1977
Kei Takei	1977
Op Odyssey	1977
How do you Feel?	1977
Dance Four	1977
Rocker	1977
Dance Three	1977
The Emperor's New Clothes	1977
Dance Ten	1977
Improvisation	1977
Melting Statues	1976
Cynthia & Squares	1976
Dance Five	1976
Gus Solomons	1975
Cynthia Anderson	1975
Jacqueline Smith-Lee	1975
Marnee Morris	1975
Rocking Orange in Three Versions	1975
Philadelphia Quartet	1975
Dance Seven	1975
Dance Nine	1975
Dance Eleven	1975
Moving Forms	1975
Squares	1974
Tall Arches	1974
Rocking Orange	1974
Moon Gates—Three Versions	1974

MICHELLE CITRON

38   Michelle Citron

Born in Boston in 1948, Michelle Citron has been teaching in the Radio-Television-Film Department at Northwestern University, Evanston, Illinois, since 1978; she is currently Associate Professor and Head of Production in the department. A graduate of the University of Massachusetts-Amherst, where she received a B.S. in 1970, Citron earned an interdisciplinary Ph.D. from the University of Wisconsin-Madison in 1974. Her work in cognition combined the disciplines of psychology, communication, and education.

Citron has received grants from The National Endowment for the Humanities, 1986; The National Endowment for the Arts, 1985 and 1981, and the Illinois Arts Council, 1985. She received The Golden Athens Award for the Best Experimental Narrative Film from the Athens International Film Festival, Athens, Ohio, in 1979, for *Daughter Rite.* Her work has been widely reviewed in journals such as *Afterimage, American Film, Jump Cut, Variety, Film Quarterly, Film Library Quarterly,* and others. E. Ann Kaplan did an analysis of Citron's films in *Women and Film: Both Sides of the Camera,* (New York and London: Methuen, 1983), in Chapter 12, and Annette Kuhn explored Citron's work in *Women's Pictures: Feminism and Cinema,* (London: Routledge and Kegan Paul, 1983), in Chapter 8 and on the cover.

Her films have been shown worldwide, including the Berlin Film Festival, the London Film Festival, the Edinburgh Film Festival, the American Film Festival, New Directors at MOMA, the Walker Arts Center, and the Art Institute of Chicago, among others. Citron's screenings and lectures include those at Wellesley College, the University of Minnesota, the

University of Rochester, New York University, The John Hopkins University, SUNY-Binghamton, the University of Chicago, Rutgers University, the University of Colorado, Indiana University, Ohio State University, and Michigan State University.

Some of her presentations are "Redefining Women's Work," a paper presented at *Viewpoints: A Conference on Women, Culture and Public Media* (a seminar on philosophy and film); "Objectivity/Subjectivity in Narrative and Documentary" for the American Museum for the Moving Image; "Documentary Filmmaking: Aesthetics and Political Questions," a symposium of women made films at Walker Art Center; "Women in Filmmaking," a symposium of women in film, number IV, at The American Film Institute; "Strategies for a More Progressive Aesthetic" at The International Feminist Film/Video Conference; and "Feminist Film Criticism in *Jump Cut*" at The Edinburgh International Film Festival, a conference on "Feminism and Film."

Michelle Citron lives in Chicago and is a member of the Association of Independent Video and Film, Women in Film/Chicago, and the Chicago Film and Video Network.

Stills from Michelle Citron's narrative film about women in non-traditional work, *What You Take for Granted . . .*, distributed by Women Make Movies. Photo credit: Frances Reid.

From *What You Take for Granted....* Photo credit: Michelle Citron.

INTERVIEW

Interview with Michelle Citron, director of *Daughter Rite* and *What You Take for Granted*..., on January 23, 1987.

M) We got a lot of money to make this new film: *Great Expectations: Life and Death in the World of High Tech Medicine.* I could have taken you out to dinner.

L) Who's funding it?

M) [We got] $20,000 from the National Endowment for the Arts, a $20,000 Planning Grant from the National Endowment for the Humanities, and $20,000 from the Kellogg Foundation. They fund a lot of medical issues; I don't think they've ever funded a film before. But Michael, one of the coproducers, has received a lot of funding for his research from the Kellogg Foundation.

L) Michael who?

M) Michael Hyde. We also got some money from Northwestern University, where I teach.

L) That's great.

M) I know. Isn't it amazing? I keep thinking this is how adults make movies. I come downtown and I can easily park because there's money to pay for it. I can go out and buy this wonderful tape recorder.

L) Are you the project director?

M) Michael is the project director. The three of us are coproducers. The three of us are going to

41

write the treatment, then I'm going to write the script for the narrative. Perhaps with one of them.

L) Who's the other person?

M) Gordon Quinn.

L) Is he a filmmaker?

M) From Kartemquin films. He makes political documentaries.

L) Have you worked with either of these people before?

M) No, I have never worked with anyone before. When I finished *What You Take for Granted* ... it ended something for me. I've had a lot of ambivalent feelings about that film.

L) You finished that in what year?

M) 1983, four years ago.

L) What did it end? I don't understand.

M) I can only talk about it in metaphor. Because I was trained as a scientist all the way through my doctorate I have a model of working that is the scientific model, which is—you do your initial experiment and while it's based upon some hypotheses, based on the reading of the literature or some model, whatever, it's a first attempt. It's a stab in the dark. And once you do the first experiment, the results narrow your focus and move you down one path or another path. What becomes important is a series of experiments and how they move you in a particular direction. No one experiment is *the* one. Whatever path I was moving down, in some way, when I finished *What You Take for*

Granted . . . it was as if I had come up against a brick wall. I needed to, not retreat—I'm not quite sure about this metaphor—but I needed to move off in another direction. I'm still working with the same issues, but I couldn't continue along the same path. *Daughter Rite* was on that path and a film I made before *Daughter Rite* called *Parthenogenesis* was on that path. That path involved different issues and one of them was that I worked by myself. I was *the* filmmaker. I was the producer, I was the director, whatever description you want to use. I totally controlled the film. I raised all the money, I was responsible for everything. Sometimes, I needed to work with other people, as in *What You Take for Granted* . . . , so I hired them, and they worked for me. The film was my responsibility in every way: conceptualization, execution, the final product. When I finished *What You Take for Granted* . . . , I didn't want to do that anymore.

L) It's almost like a large painting. You use science as model, but it's also the way a painter will work on a huge painting. She can't always do everything. You can hire people to execute certain things. . . .

M) Interesting.

L) I have a friend who is a stained glass artist. It's her piece, she designs it, but she may hire people to put certain parts in it, to cut certain elements perhaps, but she signs it, it's her signature on the piece.

M) Right, I understand that. When I finished that film I realized I had limitations. If I wanted to keep moving in the direction I was moving in, which was larger films, perhaps, I either needed to retreat and go back to making smaller films (although I'm not quite sure how to define a smaller film—smaller focus, shorter in length, slightly pulled back production values, all of that), I either needed to move backward and work smaller or to realize that I couldn't do everything, that I did some things well, I didn't do other things well, and I needed to work in collaboration. That was one of the bricks in the wall that I came up against; there were others. So it became very important to me to work in collaboration, and it's been fantastic.

L) How did you come upon this collaboration? Did they ask you? Did you ask them?

M) Michael, who teaches at Northwestern in Communication Studies, had been doing research for a number years on a W.K. Kellogg Foundation Fellowship on doctor-patient communication and how hi-tech medicine has affected it. Instead of writing a book like a "normal" academic, he decided he wanted to make a movie and so he came to me.

L) How did he connect with you?

M) Well, we're both at Northwestern, and I don't know quite how to say this. We were the "hot" young faculty members in my college, and we both got early tenure. There were certain ways within his field and department and within my field and department that made us seem like mavericks, yet we were perceived as being—I don't know what word to use, because stars isn't the right word—slightly different and exciting in some way. I knew of his existence because of it. We were always being compared to one another, as opposed to other faculty members coming up for tenure, rising in the ranks, and just plodding along in their own safe little paths. I don't know whether somebody suggested he speak with me, but he came and saw me; he had the idea that he wanted to make a film and he didn't know much about film. He was naive in a certain way, but very smart. I put him through hell for three months. I wouldn't tell him if I would work with him or not. We spent a lot of time together. I read all of his articles, and he looked at my films, and we had long talks about our work. We'd go out for lunch and have very intense conversations. I said to him, if we do this film, it's like getting married, and we'd better date first.

L) That's great. Was he seductive?

M) He was very seductive. In retrospect, I think he liked the fact that I did that; it said something about me.

L) You didn't tumble for his idea. He respected you.

M) Yes.

L) So you were trying to see if you could work well with him because it is what, an 18-month, two-year, three-year commitment?

M) Four years at least. It's a very long process, and I wanted to know if our chemistry worked. We're very different. He's very much an academic and caught up in that world in a way that I'm not.

L) What is his discipline?

M) He's in communication studies. His background is in philosophy. I am very direct and blunt, and he is very politic. I am very political (from the antiwar movement of the 1960s and feminism) and I live a certain kind of lifestyle in the inner city. He's married, lives in the North Shore suburbs, and is not political in any way at all. But he's intelligent and well read in a way that I'm not. I have the politics, but he understands the Marxist theory. And he's very open and flexible.

L) What was his reaction when he saw *Daughter Rite* and *What You Take for Granted. . .?*

M) He liked them a lot.

L) He understood . . .

M) Well, he didn't understand theoretically what I was doing but . . .

L) How about communication? Did he understand the communication?

M) He understood the communication. The project he's working on now is about modernism so he understands the concept of realism, modernism, and manipulation of form. But he didn't have any experience with film other than going to the local movie theater. He didn't have the language of film theory, but he certainly understood issues about subjectivity and discourse and voice and rhetoric. He understood why I did not work in a very slick way, and he understood about the emotional texture of a film. There was no problem at all. He is a very sophisticated, intelligent viewer even though he only knows film rhetoric.

L) How was he about the distinctly feminist flavor? What did he think about that?

M) It was fine. He's married to a woman who is one tough woman; it's fine. And so, I said yes, I want to work on this project but there are a few things I want. One is that I want to direct. And I want to be a coproducer. I also want it to be a mixture of documentary and narrative fiction. I spent a lot of time during that two- or three-month period convincing him why I thought this approach was important for this particular subject.

L) Did he have reservations about that, even after seeing your films?

M) No. I said, "I'm not a documentary film-maker; if we're going to do this, we have to bring in somebody else." There are two documentary film-makers in Chicago who make up Kartemquin Films: Gordon Quinn and Jerry Blumenthal. They've been making political documentary films for 20 years. I told Michael, "I'm not a documentary filmmaker; bring in this group," although ulti-mately only Gordon is working on the film. It's complicated, because of course the question was: Is this group going to come in for hire to work under us, or are we bringing in one more partner? That took more time to figure out. Ultimately, Gordon became a coproducer and the director of the docu-mentary, I'm a coproducer and director of the nar-rative, and Michael is a coproducer and the project director. Gordon was excited about the idea of a documentary and narrative fiction mix. At this point, it's not just my formulation. It's the work of the three of us. If you're talking about hi-tech medicine, if you're talking about the relationship of our culture to technology, one way to present it is through an analytic documentary, which is the dominant form of political documentary in this country since the 1960s. It is usually film that is some combination of cinema vérité with analysis, with a small bit of voice-over narration. That is a good form to present and analyze certain kinds of issues—economic issues, political issues—but medicine is more emotionally charged, in part because it's about life and death. People can make a theoretical decision never to go on a respirator, but when it comes down to that moment, they really can't predict what they'll decide. I think that what people decide before they get sick is sometimes what they still want once they are sick, but not always. The emotional turmoil makes actions unpredictable.

L) That's true. Ultimately, I think people really want to live and are driven to do a lot of things.

M) And things that they would tell you that they would never do. Some people, like your aunt, did something different.

L) She had made her decision and she wished she could just go click and be gone. It wasn't so easy to just die. Her body wanted to stay alive.

M) I thought that narrative fiction and not documentary was the best way to explore the psychological and emotional texture of being in the hi-tech medicine world. And that documentary was essential for presenting the political issues. The film needed to move in and out of these two different filmic approaches.

L) It reminds me of two ways of doing science, especially in the social sciences, quantitative and qualitative.

M) Right, the topic needs multiple perspectives. And then there are other issues. When you talk about hi-tech medicine, you're talking about people dying, and we have moral and ethical concerns about bringing in a camera and sticking it in somebody's face. I go into the hospital and I think, here's a family gathered around a dying person and this is more important than a film I'm making. And there's the issue of voyeurism. If we show a documentary image of a person dying, the audience is caught up in the fact that they are watching a real person die, when the point of the scene might be something else—for example, what kind of decision was made for treatment or who made that decision.

L) Let's talk a minute about what you mean by narrative, and how you work. Tell me about how you construct a narrative. You don't sit down in your office and make it up.

M) What do I know about hi-tech medicine? What do I know about dying? Very little. I don't have a disease; it's not my own experience. The narrative needs to be generated from the data (Michael calls it the "data"). It needs to come from real experience. That's how I generated both *Daughter Rite* and *What You Take for Granted*. . . . In both of those films I interviewed a lot of women. It was not sociologically rigid. I was a very active participant in those interviews and I heard a lot of stories. I also saw characters. I think that I work from what's out there. It's not all in my head; it's not all in me. It somehow comes through me, and that's why I need to interview people. This film has to be tied to the real world and the experience lived in a way that seems much more crucial than my other films, even *What You Take for Granted* . . . , which is a very rhetorical film. The interviews are necessary to help make decisions about characters and situations. Does going through the experience of the disease (whether the character lives or dies is not even the central issue), does it become a transcending experience? Is it an experience where the character learns something, becomes a different person, a more whole person? Or does it destroy the character? Is there a way in which the ego can't come to terms with the experience? That happens, too. I need to interview people and get stories and characters to understand.

L) You gather the stories and the characters, and then you have, I imagine, lots of hours of tapes. So then what do you do? Do you transcribe?

M) Oh, yes, I transcribe all the tapes; it gives me something concrete to work with.

L) Words on paper.

M) Words on paper, styles, and the way people talk. It's very clear from our interviewing that there's one person that I want to make a character in the film. There's a particular way in which he spoke, a particular relationship between what he was saying and how he was acting that was very complex. The story is out there and I pull it from the world instead of creating it exclusively in my head. There needs to be a synthesis between the world and my imagination. Maybe that's a better way to talk about it. So far, working with these two men has not changed this process. All the "I's" are just "we's."

L) But in both films you end up with only a few. In *Daughter Rite* you end up with two characters.

M) One reason for interviewing is so that I can sift out common experiences, using the model of the consciousness-raising group—certain common experiences become themes that I recognize as important to weave into the film. Now, once I get all those common experiences together, the experiences themselves might suggest a character, and sometimes they do, and in some of my films that's how characters evolved. The character is suddenly there. And once I have the character, the character takes on a life of its own; some of the experiences I collected I have to throw out because they just don't fit into the particular character. I can talk about *Daughter Rite*. I realized that there were some women who were trying to puzzle out their relationship with their mothers with a certain degree of self-awareness. And there were other women who just spewed out stories without any awareness at all. And that was what was behind the two types of characters. One type was represented by the narrator in the film and the other was represented by the two sisters in the "documentary." In *What You Take for Granted* . . . it was very clear there were working-class women, there were professional women. There were women who were very fragmented, there were women who were much more integrated. To be an artist means certain kinds of things, to be a carpenter, to do that kind of job which is hourly work and trade-unionized, is a different kind of work. I made those kinds of analyses based upon the interviews I did.

L) I think *Daughter Rite* and *What You Take for Granted* . . . are personal for you, involved with issues in your own life, but this time I don't know if it's as personal for you as the others. How has that affected the way you're working? What is the new film called?

M) It's called *Great Expectation: Life and Death in the World of High Tech Medicine.*

L) How is it personal for you, or does that not matter anymore? Have you gotten beyond that?

M) No, it's very personal to me.

L) Not because you're ill, you don't have an illness.

M) It's personal on a much subtler level. I guess this has to do with Hollywood, too, because when I finished *What You Take for Granted* . . . , I was very successful by my own standards. I grew up in a working-class family. I have more education than anybody in my family. I have first cousins who dropped out of high school when they were sixteen years old and ride motorcycles and I have a few cousins who went to college.

L) But you're Dr. Citron.

M) Right. When I finished *What You Take for Granted* . . . , I was far beyond what I ever fantasized I would do with my life in terms of achievement judged by myself and the external world. And

I had been very content and happy with my life. So, I thought, now what? I struggled with whether I wanted to continue to make independent films or make something that was more commercial—a theatrical feature. I think it was a battle between internal motivations and external motivations; I was very confused. I had always put my career first and I felt that the values I had lived with all my life had worked, but suddenly they weren't working anymore. For me, the focus at this point in the film's process is with the narrative fiction and the psychological, and because I work with these two other people, I don't have to worry about the politics—that's very crude, because I care very much about the politics. But I know that I don't have to be responsible for everything because Gordon and Michael are there. I can focus on what I do best—the personal and the psychological. There is something about the different ways in which people deal with a long-term debilitating or life-threatening illness that I'm learning about. I don't know how else to describe it. What I'm saying seems very abstract.

L) Not at all. It connects you with fellow human beings.

M) It connects me and sometimes I feel that this is really cheap; I get to work this out vicariously.

L) I have always thought of *Daughter Rite* and *What You Take for Granted* . . . as feminist films. I use them as models of feminist practice, not only feminist content, but a feminist way of working, because you interview a lot of women to find out their lives, collectivizing their experiences, and then shape characters out of the material. Do you think that the way you're working now with this collaboration is still a feminist way of working? Do you think this is a feminist approach? How do you feel about it? Or is that a silly question?

M) It's not a silly question. It's the same way I've always worked, which has to do with trying to be—not always successfully—receptive to what other people are telling me and having that enter into my consciousness as I make a film, as opposed to my having an idea and going out and imposing it on the world. In that sense, my style is absolutely the same and I've always thought of it as feminist.

L) Even though the issues now are different. Health care is a feminist issue, but not many people see it as one.

M) It is. I am working with men who are very open to the way I work, and they're working the same way I am. We work together. Part of it is because Gordon is a documentary filmmaker, and there's a way in which his style of documentary filmmaking has always been very process oriented— filmmaking as a mode of inquiry. But an issue of the film is whether the patient will be a woman or a man. Is the doctor going to be a woman or a man? How does gender work in the dynamics of the doctor-patient relationship? Issues about medicine and power. Those all become very conscious decisions that will have to be made. It's clear that the sex of all the characters has to be carefully thought out, just as the race has to be, and other issues like that. I don't think to be feminist you have to make films just about "women's" issues. Women comprise 53 percent of the population; we're talking about health care. I think it's a very feminist issue. I like the idea of my work opening up in some way. That's part of what this film is for me, opening up. I think that if my life had moved in a different direction, if I was making theatrical narrative films based on the Hollywood model, then I don't think that I could work the same way. But I don't know.

L) Are you saying that because no one has ever done a Hollywood script that way before? You're talking about generating a script after you interview a lot of people.

M) No, I think people can generate a script that way. But I do not have any pressures to generate a script that will result in a film that will fit certain expectations of the commercial marketplace. I suspect that *Great Expectations* is going to be a narrative fiction film, but it's not going to be a narrative that necessarily has the same flow or the same structure as a theatrical narrative fiction film, particularly since it's going to have a documentary woven through it.

L) I think I understand. But how is it going to be different from something everyone experiences on television, for example on "St. Elsewhere," where they have real issues and experiences?

M) That's a good question. "St. Elsewhere" is very good at dealing with a specific issue. This week they deal with malpractice, the next week they deal with kids who have anxiety attacks over the nuclear bomb, another week they deal with what happens if you are in the hospital and don't have the money to pay for it. You sell your home and totally destroy your life savings so that you can go on welfare to get government economic support for your medical care. It's about individual issues. What *Great Expectations* is trying to say is you cannot separate out any one issue. We're going to look at all 20 variables simultaneously. High-tech medicine presents a huge contradiction and paradox, and most of us don't enter into this world with that realization.

L) That insurance part is very important. You need a secretary to do all the paperwork. There's a pile of forms, bills; you have to be healthy to deal with all that. I'm serious. Are you going to do something on insurance in this film?

M) Yes, yes, of course. One of the things that happens is that people make a decision to live at all costs, and that cost will sometimes destroy the family, economically destroy the family, and then they die. People will sell their homes, and there are a lot of people who have to go on welfare to get their medical care paid for, which means that they have to sell everything, destroy everything, before they can do that. Yes, that is part of it. So my argument is that on a program like "St. Elsewhere," you see all these problems in isolation, but you don't understand how they all interrelate. And how, once you enter the system, you have to deal with everything simultaneously; that's what makes it so difficult. I don't think that "St. Elsewhere" contextualizes the melodrama. It's really good at melodrama, but it doesn't contextualize it. That's the difference.

L) Is your theory of filmmaking changing with this new experience? It sounds as if it is. You said that you had come to the end of a period in your life, the completion of *What You Take for Granted* . . . ended one path, and you started on a new path of collaboration. Yet you're doing the narrative structure in the way you worked before. How are you discovering something new about yourself—about your way of working—by doing this new film?

M) Well, if you use the scientific model, once you hit a dead end with an experiment, you don't just jump over to a new discipline. You go back to the last juncture in the path, to the fork, and you go up another branch of the fork. I don't get rid of my past; it's all one long continuous process. It's just that I went down a path—a tributary—that didn't lead anywhere, and I needed to readjust. I didn't answer your question. Ask your question again in a different way.

L) From what you've told me about this new work, you're making discoveries about yourself as you work and things are evolving for you simultaneously as you make the new film. You don't know yet exactly what direction it will take.

M) That's how I've always worked. And that's what *Daughter Rite* was for me. Filmmaking is very personal and very psychological. I criticize filmmakers who use films as therapy and say they should go to a shrink instead of dumping their psychoses on the screen, but I'm not talking about it at that level. I interview people so that I hope I avoid that. There is something very therapeutic to me about the process of filmmaking. Filmmaking is the way through which I grow as a person, psychologically, politically, and personally. It's the way in which I find out something about myself in relation to others and the world. For instance, I discover that when I interview people now, I do it very differently than when I interviewed people for *Daughter Rite*. And that difference says something about how I've changed as a person in a way that I think is positive. If I'm not learning something about myself in the process of making a film, I get very bored and I don't want to do it. Sometimes what I learn has to do with how I interact with colleagues. Sometimes what I learn has to do with how I direct a crew of twelve people. Sometimes what I learn is how I'm stuck on this film and I'm editing it, and I don't know what I'm doing and I'm really scared. Or I've been editing a film for nine months and it should have taken a month and a half and it's because I'm too scared to finish it and have it out there and publicly criticized. I learned that four or five films ago. I have to learn something else on this film and from working on this project that's bigger than women, that includes women, but is more; it's big enough for me to learn something new.

L) It's clearing new spaces.

M) That's a nice metaphor.

L) You said that you had studied to be a scientist. You have a Ph.D. in . . . ?

M) Cognitive psychology. Cognition and perception.

L) And you didn't become a shrink.

M) No, it's not shrink psychology; it's research psychology. I wrote my dissertation on how the brain organizes and synthesizes stimuli.

L) Ways of knowing.

M) Ways of knowing. And now I'm just exploring the same thing in a different way.

L) Where did you pick up film along this path?

M) I did my graduate work on how we process multiple channels of information, and the stimuli I used were visual and auditory stimuli. I made very complicated slide shows that had nine simultaneous screens and three simultaneous channels of audio information, and I would reorder the information and give it to a control group in linear fashion and to experimental groups in different kinds of simultaneous structures. I'd take all this information and feed it into a computer and do multiple variant analyses to try to figure out what was going on. It was ridiculous.

L) No, it sounds fascinating.

M) It wasn't. It was so ridiculous because the methodology—the statistical methodology—was not appropriate, was way too simplified for the complexity of the phenomena that I was trying to study. I was not satisfied with studying phenomena that were appropriate for the methodology and there was no methodology, at the time at least, to study the phenomena at the complexity that I wanted to study. I was in a department that was very behavioristic—this was in the late 1960s, early 1970s—and that was very limiting. My advisor said to me, "You're making all of these visual stimuli; you don't know anything about making images. Why don't you take a film course?" So I begged my way into a film course. The instructor was influenced by what was happening at the end of the 1960s and beginning of the 1970s in terms of student-centered education.

L) Where were you?

M) University of Wisconsin in Madison. The instructor, a man named Jim Heddle, was very important to me. He taught a class that used super 8mm film. It met on Friday afternoons from 12 to 5. We walked into the classroom and for five hours we watched experimental film. When the films were over, Heddle would stand in front of the class and wait for us to respond. And nobody would say anything and then the class would be over. I had never experienced anything like this.

L) What did he show you?

M) Everything. Will Hindle, Stan Brackage, Bruce Baille, Norm McLaren, Maya Deren, Jordan Belson, everyone. You name it, he showed it. Leger, Buñuel. I had never seen anything like this in my life, had never, ever seen anything like this in my life.

L) Talk about visual stimuli.

M) I know. And I thought—whoa—because I had seen only Hollywood movies. I was getting involved in the women's movement at the time, and was frustrated with psychology, particularly since behaviorism was the only way to do it. So it all came together, and I thought, I want to be a filmmaker. I always wanted to be a creative person. I always wanted to do something in art, but I never had a voice. I can't draw, I have no musical talent.

My sister's a musician, but I have no musical talent. I cannot write. I actually think I can write now, but I always believed I couldn't write. I thought, here's my language. I was really frustrated with psychology, and I was getting involved in the women's movement and I was getting political. I was very much radicalized. It started in college in the 1960s in the antiwar movement. Then I went to Wisconsin and there were buildings being bombed. And I thought, I'm going to make movies—I can make movies, I can be an artist. And I can have politics and I can just chuck psychology.

L) But you didn't chuck psychology.

M) Well, I was so close to getting my doctorate, and I'm always very practical. But I've never used my psychology education.

L) But you're still thinking about some of the issues in cognition and perception and how to understand the world.

M) I do, but you know, when I wrote my dissertation, I cheated. I knew I wanted to get a Ph.D. I thought I had to—I wanted to—yet I couldn't do another experiment. I was working on a complicated experiment, and felt I couldn't do it anymore. So, I petitioned the university to grant me an interdisciplinary doctorate. I wrote my dissertation on the philosophy of knowledge in art and science as different modes of inquiry, as different ways of organizing reality. It was based on what at that time was known about the split-brain split-hemisphere research, which was part of cognition at that point. I made a short film as part of my dissertation. The dissertation was about the multiplicity of perspectives and how no one rhetoric explains it all. Now I make films that are a documentary and narrative mixture. That was a pivotal point in my life and I do the same thing now, but I do it in film.

L) I'm interested that you do use an experimental technique. Doing all the interviews is research, almost scientific research.

M) That's different. I think that I have something inside of me; artists supposedly say that, right? That they have something inside of them. But it only works when it gets stimulated by something outside.

L) I think different artists say different things. Some artists say I paint what I see out there and some say I paint what I feel, and some do a blend.

M) It's both. Some kind of synthesis, maybe.

L) You are one of the first filmmakers I have talked to who doesn't have a specific background in art. Most of the filmmakers I've interviewed came out of dance, painting, architecture, had different kinds of art training. I think it's very interesting that you see yourself as a scientist.

M) Isn't it? It's very weird.

L) Do you think that it makes a difference in any way that you're a woman, that the films you make are different because you're a woman, or do you think that gender doesn't matter?

M) I think it really matters. Are you asking if I think it's socialization, acculturation versus essentialism? Are you asking that?

L) Could be, I don't know if I'm asking that.

M) Because that question I can't answer. I tend to be too much of a materialist to believe that it's essentialist.

L) I don't think that it's essentialist, either.

M) So that I can't answer. Yes, I think my being a woman does affect things.

L) Do you make films differently, or different films, because of gender?

M) Sure. I sit in a different place in the culture than a man does. I was very much formed by the women's movement because of my age. It happened at a very formative time in my life—when I went off to college—and I can't separate any of that out of myself. The women's movement happened simultaneously with my decision to become a filmmaker. I was always, always concerned with ethical issues: the relationship between the filmmaker and the subject of the documentary film or the relationship between the filmmaker and the film and the audience or the relationship between art and politics. So I was formed by that moment in history which included the women's movement. But I'm not sure that a black filmmaker might not say something similar. That he or she was formed by the black political movement, the historic moment of the 1960s, even starting in the 1950s. I can't separate any of that; I'm so much a part of my culture.

L) Do you have a network of other women filmmakers that you talk to or other filmmakers, men or women?

M) Yes, I do have a network of other film-makers that I talk to. But in fact the network also includes film critics, women who are doing theoretical work, especially since I'm in an academic setting. I talk to lots of other filmmakers.

L) Do you show your work to one another?

M) Oh, yes. Even when I worked by myself, I always got feedback at many stages in the process.

L) Do you have a formal structure for that? Do you have meetings where you show each other work in progress?

M) No, no.

L) You just call and say come over and look at this piece?

M) "You've got to come over and give me feedback; I'm going nuts. I'm going to break my movieola if you don't come over and help me." Yes, it's like that and it's back and forth all the time and it's with women and sometimes, men. I live in Chicago and there aren't that many women filmmakers in Chicago, though there are some. But we're not really close. We make very different kinds of films; we're friendly with each other, we support each other, but we're not friends. There's one woman in particular I'm very close friends with, who works in the industry as an A.C. and her love is making films with the Kwakuit'l Indians in British Columbia, the Indians who were filmed by Boas. He taught them media so now they're making their own films and tapes.

L) Who is that?

M) Her name is Judy Hoffman.

L) Oh, yes. She's given them the technology.

M) Right. They're very political. They're organized and political as a culture. I'm very close to her—I work closely with her. And I have a friend who's a screenwriter in the city, Karin Pritken, who works on very traditional films. Chuck Kleinhanst and Julia Lesage are here. I teach with Chuck, and then there are the people at Kartemquin.

L) Are you involved with Women in the Director's Chair at all?

M) No.

L) You'd show if they should ask you?

M) Sure. And I know them. They would help me out if I needed it, and I would help them out if they needed it, but we just go our own ways. That's very strange, isn't it?

L) No, not strange.

M) Typical, maybe.

L) So, to a degree, you said you needed collaboration, but you are also still working alone in some ways.

M) No, because of this collaboration, I'm not working alone. We meet twice a week and we go to the hospital and we observe together all the time and we share ideas—the script ideas and character ideas—and then we go off and write and come back. No, it's really a collaboration.

L) Have your parents understood your involvement in film and the women's movement and been supportive of it?

M) Yes, my parents are supportive. There's a level at which my parents are excited for me because I am successful. They're excited and they get caught up in it and they love me and it's wonderful. My parents are divorced.

L) Yes, I learned that in *Daughter Rite*.

M) My father lives with a woman my age, someone with whom he has lived for ten years, who is very self-aware. My mother works in a gay bar and restaurant in Hawaii and is very active in something called the Life Foundation, which is a support educational group for people with AIDS. My parents are working-class people.

L) They're working class but they understand intellectual aspiration . . .

M) That's because they're Jewish.

L) I didn't know that.

M) I'm Jewish. That explains everything. One of my great-grandfathers was a *rebbe*. I was very close to all four of my grandparents because they were all alive until I was in my twenties and I grew up in an extended family with two of them. I lived with my mother's parents and my own parents. My grandfather, my father's father, never went to school, but he was a very educated man, a self-educated man. My parents love the fact that I teach at a university and have a Ph.D. They have their own lives and they lead active lives. The point—the important point—is that my parents have never stopped growing themselves. My parents got divorced, my mother moved to Hawaii, and she started a new life. She's just joined the Toastmaster's Club. It's something that I would never do because it's from a different time and a different culture, but she's joined the Toastmaster's Club. She's learning how to make public speeches and she's excited and she tells me her speeches. And she works with people with AIDS. My father decided that he's going back to school and takes classes in computers. And they're really supportive of me. Neither of my parents is a judgmental person at all, in any way.

L) And they see all your work?

M) They see all my work but what they care about is that I'm happy. Neither one of them is materialistic and their priorities are very much those of health and happiness. Literally. Isn't it amazing? I like both my parents a lot.

L) And you have a sister.

M) I have a sister who's a musician. She's a classical violinist except now she plays in a Klesmer band. Do you know what a Klesmer band is?

L) Isn't that Yiddish music?

M) Yes, Yiddish music from the shtetl, and it's wonderful music. It's very joyous music. And she teaches the Suzuki method; she's a violinist.

L) Have you ever toyed with the idea of doing a film on your Jewish roots or does that not interest you at all?

M) I was married when I was very young to a

man who almost became a rabbi, and I was very active in organized religion when I was a kid and growing up. It was the center of my social life. My husband ran a very large religious school for a while. I think that that experience was very important to me, it was very formative in some way, but it's as if it was somebody else's life. There's some way in which I don't know how to reconnect it to my life in the present; maybe I will in the future. I don't know.

L) Adrienne Rich did that in her poetry, she decided to go back and pick up some of the strands.

M) The strands are there, and they were so important and such a focus of my life for so long. From the time I was 19 to the time I was 23, I taught religious school. This is a deep secret. It was important, but it hasn't been for years, and at some point, I suspect the strand will be picked up in some way and woven back into my life. I don't know how. Actually, I've always thought that my politics came from my Judaism and the particular congregation that I grew up in, which was very political.

L) Are you from the Chicago area?

M) No, I'm from Boston. It was very political, and the emphasis was always on social action and social issues, in the same way that a lot of churches now are very political. I think that that made me open and receptive to the 1960s and the political movements—the civil rights movement, the anti-war movement, the women's movement.

L) Tell me a little bit about your teaching. You teach film. How did you get into teaching film, and who are your students and what has become of them?

M) I have a Ph.D., so what you do? You teach. Nobody cared that I had a Ph.D. in cognitive psychology; all they cared was that I had a Ph.D., and my very first teaching job was teaching film and television at Temple University.

L) This was when? Had you made some films before you began at Temple?

M) Yes, I had made a couple of short avant-garde films and was in the process of making *Parthenogenesis,* a half-hour film. I could demonstrate to them that I had the skills and I got the job. They were desperate to have a woman. I found out later that they had three suits filed against them for discriminating against women—not the department, but the university—the department had never had a woman, and they were desperate to get a woman in there and it was a horrible job. I was very young. At the time, I did not know how to handle what it meant to be the woman breaking the barrier. There were a lot of reasons why it was not a good job for me.

L) Did you know Wanda Bershon when you were at Temple? Was she there?

M) No, but I sure know that name. Who is she?

L) She teaches film, not filmmaking, but film criticism and communication.

M) No, she came after me. I taught there in 1974. I taught with another woman; they hired us together. We were the first women they ever had in the department.

L) And you left.

M) And we left. I left after one year. I felt like a failure even though I chose to leave. I broke my contract; I had a tenure track position. I went to a small experimental college in Grand Rapids, Michigan. It was called William James College; it's no longer in existence. It was part of Grand Valley State Colleges which is part of the state university college system. It was a wonderful college, run by the faculty and students. It's like Evergreen State College. There were no departments and no grades. Half the faculty were women and I was there for three years. It was just what I wanted to do. I needed to get out of traditional academia. But in my filmmaking I was pretty isolated. There was no community. There was a woman filmmaker who taught at the college but she wasn't actively working on anything at the time. I was living with a man who was also a filmmaker but we were very isolated. I started *Daughter Rite* there. That's where I did all the interviews and shot and cut the film. As I worked on that film, I came to Chicago every chance I could. It was a three-and-a-half-hour drive, and I would come once a month; I would hang out with people here.

M) To film?

M) I came to see people. Ruby Rich was living here; Chuck Kleinhanst and Julia Lesage were here, and *Jump Cut*. There was a community. Now that I'm here, I know there's no community, but it felt to me then . . .

L) It felt as if there was, when you were in Grand Rapids, Michigan.

M) Right, and I understand why all these people come here. It felt as if there was a community here and I could come and have conversations about films.

L) I know the Art Institute has a film program, and they show wonderful films on a regular basis.

M) And Chicago Filmmakers is a great exhibition space for showing films. There was activity here, and I was starving for it. It was very hard teaching at this college because it was very labor intensive, since it had an experimental structure. The school didn't run itself.

L) Everybody had to do everything.

M) Everybody had to do everything all the time, and I was making *Daughter Rite* . . .

L) Sort of like the women's movement.

M) Right, just like the women's movement. You don't have a hierarchy, you don't have job distinctions, and everybody does everything. I was going crazy. Actually, there was something else going on, too. I was involved in a very tight-knit group of women who were very political—feminist political—and very involved in "goddess" stuff and women's spirituality, and I spent all my time with them. They were my community toward the end.

L) Why do you hate the "goddess" stuff?

M) I'm going to tell you. They all started buying houses in the ghetto and becoming absentee landlords. It drove me crazy that they could have feminist politics, but were cut off from all other kinds of politics. I started to feel very critical, and had to get out of there.

L) You questioned their integrity.

M) Not all of them, but there were enough, and Grand Rapids is a very strange place.

L) I have a cousin in Cadillac, is that near?

M) No, it's not. Grand Rapids is very Calvinist—all Dutch-Christian Reformed—and that creates an atmosphere that affects everything else, including women's issues there. It's an ultra-conservative city, and I started to feel crazy. I was working on *Daughter Rite* and started to feel that this film was important, that this film was different from all the other films I had made, and I had to get out of there. I applied for every job I found out about and was offered the job at Northwestern. It was a fantasy come true. I was able to move to Chicago; I didn't have to commute there anymore. So I came here and that's where I've been teaching ever since—nine years.

L) Why do you think that it's good to teach at Northwestern?

M) The reason I decided to go to Northwestern was because I wanted to be with a university that was a very traditional university, that seemingly ran itself, that was a research institution where they valued research and I would have a lighter teaching load. I was in the classroom 18 to 22 hours a week at Grand Valley and at Northwestern I'm in the classroom 7 to 8 hours a week. That's a big difference. Because Northwestern has a very strong emphasis on research, the teaching load reflects that. I have a lot more freedom. I give up a lot, too. I teach in an institution where I have no control, as opposed to Grand Valley, where I had a lot of control. That was very important at that point in my life. It became more important for me to be a filmmaker than an academic even though I care about teaching.

L) At Northwestern do you get to use certain resources for your own work?

M) Yes, I get to use certain resources for my own work, and I have a lot of autonomy in what I want to teach—a lot. I can teach anything I want. I mean, I clearly have certain responsibilities to the department and they're important to me in terms of teaching production courses, but from the moment I walked in there I taught women's courses in the film department and they've always been supportive, in terms of money for renting films or whatever. It has never been a issue. The women students in the department are very organized.

L) Do they have a film collection that they own?

M) A very small collection, it's never been a priority. I teach feminist film history, theory, and criticism, but since I've been there, other women have been hired. There's a woman, Mimi White, who is in theory and criticism, and since she's been there, we alternate teaching the course and I like that. I mainly teach production. I teach production and production, production, production. That's what I teach. I also teach a graduate course in aesthetics.

L) Oh, that's good.

M) I like that a lot.

L) When you teach production, do you think you have a different way of working? How do you work when you teach production?

M) I wrote an article about teaching production, and how I thought I did it differently because I was a woman, how I was very conscious of women in the classroom, and how I'd try to present the material in a way that would be accessible for women who had the inclination to have the material be accessible. I wrote it with Ellen Seiter who was there with me at the time, teaching production.

L) Where was it published?

M) It was published in *Jump Cut.*

L) But you told me something interesting before, that in the beginning classes you have 50-50.

M) Yes, men and women, and by the senior year, the classes are almost all men. This year, I'm teaching a graduate class and I'd say less than a third of the students are women.

L) So they have an M.F.A. in filmmaking?

M) Yes, they have an M.F.A. in filmmaking.

L) That's good to know. Do they teach film and video or just film?

M) Oh, it's great. I like the program a lot. The first course is a combination production and theory course, and they learn about semiotics, although we never use that word at that point, but they do learn how to read an image, and they learn a lot about aesthetics as well as production in their freshman year. Then they take a course in aesthetics, but it's done through production. They have to shoot a film every two weeks. They're given a list of contents and a list of formal aspects; each film must contain an element from each of the two lists.

L) This is the graduate course?

M) No, this is an undergraduate course. Every two weeks their films are critiqued. That's all that happens in that class and they learn a lot from it. Then, beyond that, there's no difference between the undergraduate and graduate curricula. There's a production class in video, which is a very technically oriented class. There's a production class in film which is a very technically oriented class, but in upper courses there's no distinction made between film and video. A student can take a class in documentary production, narrative production, directing, and can shoot and post in any format— video or film. The only time it makes a difference is in experimental because then we have computer animation and computer-assisted video or optical printing in film.

L) That's good.

M) Yes, it's wonderful. Also, the M.F.A. students have to take history, theory, criticism, and all the Ph.D. students have to take production.

L) Oh, that's wonderful.

M) There's a real desire for integration. The

production faculty can teach nonproduction courses and the nonproduction faculty sometimes teaches production class, particularly the beginning ones. It's a very clear program with a rationale behind it.

L) Among the graduate students, do you also have more men than women toward the end?

M) I don't know. I'd say a few more men. More men work in film but more women work in video. My speculation here is that with television—not video, but television—the women students want to become TV producers, and the men want to become film directors. I think it has to do with myths about the film director. A director is a macho thing—technology and virtuosity and control. Big budgets and special effects and seventy-millimeter—you know—the artist in a kind of large, technical, male way. The power in television is the producer, not the director, and the producer is a position that has a lot of responsibility and a lot of power, but is cut off from the actual hands-on technical stuff. It's the T.D., the technical director, and the director who actually do the technical stuff in television and they have little power. I think it has something to do with the relationship between power and technology. It's not that the women don't want the power, but they are comfortable with power that's slightly removed from technology in television.

L) I thought it might have something to do with television seeming to be a more intimate medium.

M) More intimate medium? It might.

L) Is there anything else you want to tell me that we haven't covered?

M) No, we've covered everything.

L) Thank you, I've learned a lot.

CHRONOLOGY

KAVERY DUTTA

Photo credit: Bhupender Kaul.

Kavery Dutta was born in Calcutta, India, on October 19, 1952. She lives and works in New York City and is the founder of her own production company called Riverfilms. She has a B.A. in English from Harvard University (1972).

Dutta has had extensive experience in both commercial and independent film production. Her work has been broadcast on PBS television and exhibited in film festivals throughout the world.

She has won awards at the International Latin American Film Festival and the Festival of Films on Art in Italy. Her work has been shown at the Berlin Film Festival and her other credits include an Academy Award nomination and a Dupont-Columbia Citation for Excellence in Broadcast Journalism.

Kavery is now completing a feature documentary on calypso music and the screenplay for her first dramatic film.

INTERVIEW

The following is an interview with filmmaker Kavery Dutta, who produced and directed *First Look*. The interview is dated April 6, 1983 (and was updated April 16, 1987).

L) Where are you from?

K) I was born in India, in Calcutta, where I lived until I was six, when my family moved to the United States.

L) How long have you been in films?

K) I've been in the film business for over ten years now. I started as a film editor and have been producing and directing since 1981.

L) That's interesting. That's another career path that many women take; some women stay in editing.

K) It's true that a number of women have gone into editing. That's something to be proud of since editing is so crucial to the making of any film, to understanding it. I never saw editing as a "woman's job."
As for using editing as a first step to directing, I think women tend to approach filmmaking with the feeling that they'd better know what they're doing. If you know how it all fits together in the end, you're better equipped to deal with what may seem to be a hopelessly fragmented process in the beginning. At least that was my rationale. Of course, you have to remember that a number of recognized

male directors also began as editors—David Lean, John Avildsen, Karel Reisz.

In fact, at a recent film festival in Italy, a French director said to me, "You started as an editor? That's the best way to begin a directing career." Of course, in our society, the emphasis is so much on "making it"—on what Andy Warhol once predicted as everyone being a star for fifteen minutes—that we've lost our understanding of process in our race for results. Films are big business with an alarming emphasis on hype, even in the independent world.

L) But why do you think so many women start as editors? Is it internal, psychological, or is it something out there in the business world?

K) Certainly editing was one of the first important areas of the film business to open its doors to women. People in cinematography are just starting to accept that women can handle heavy equipment and the pressures of production. The directing door will open next. And last will be producing, which will allow women to be in charge of the money.

A lot of attitudes toward women have changed. *We've* changed them. But sometimes, beneath the surface, you see leftover ways of looking at us that reflect how long it will take to change things completely. And how many generations. Because we can provoke, instigate, legislate change, but it takes generations to really put that change into effect.

Sometimes, you walk into a lab, a film equipment house, a postproduction service—and the first thing you trigger off is someone's story about a neurotic woman who was there last year, a woman who didn't know what she was doing. "I'll never forget that lady. She drove us crazy. That was sometime last year, I think. . . ." The story isn't directly aimed at you. Nor is the person unfriendly toward you, but when a male director walks in, he certainly doesn't trigger off stories about the one male who messed up.

L) Or all the many men. The "corpses" of failed male film directors litter, I'm sure, every film-making center. Not their literal corpses. It seems that women are not allowed to fail. They had better know what they're doing. We have to demonstrate more competence because we're not given the benefit of the doubt.

K) Exactly. You have no room to fail, or you'll become one of those stories of the lady who drove them crazy. You have to stay constantly on your toes and know what you're doing. I think the same experience happens to racial minorities. As an Indian-American, I trigger off everyone's stories of the one Indian they've met or even just seen from a distance. Or, sometimes, what they thought of the movie *Gandhi.* It's not necessarily malicious. It's a random association that, like most things that are so random, can work either way.

So as an Indian-American woman, I get two stories for the price of one.

L) But is that necessarily a negative thing or is it perhaps a positive thing?

K) The fact that you have to know more about what you're doing? I don't know if it's positive or negative. It's certainly something I'm aware of, but more as part of the process of changing traditional concepts, not as something that gets in the way of my filmmaking. When you go out there and you're directing a film, no director knows everything about every aspect of film. It's a medium which requires collaboration of a number of specialists to give life to the vision of the director. I've seen, though, if a male director asks a question, the question is answered, taking for granted that, of course, he may not know about the splicer or one particular light or whatever. If a woman asks the question of a male technician, it can become the basis for a long lecture, explaining in great detail not so much the one thing the woman director needed to know but all the things the man knows.

L) Did you have those types of experiences when you were making your film? Is this your first film?

K) *First Look* is my first film as producer and director. I've edited a number of films. I was associate producer on another film, *Americas in Transition*, a half-hour film on Central America, which was nominated for an Academy Award.

I don't want to paint a terrible picture of everybody attacking women all the time. We've come a long way and a lot of people made a conscious effort to be supportive while I was making *First Look.* That, in itself, is one of our successes, that we've been able to make men more aware of the necessity of reexamining traditional attitudes toward women. Of course, awareness is only a first step. We'll still sometimes get those long lectures in response to our questions. And sometimes we may even choose to quietly listen to those lectures.

L) What would happen if you would say, shut

up, I know what I'm talking about. A male director might say something like that.

K) You have to handle the situation differently. If you were to say, shut up, I know what I'm talking about, the reaction would probably be, oh, she's neurotic or becoming hysterical. But remember that, male or female, the collaborative effort that goes into the making of a film comes from a number of sensitive egos, made even more fragile by the pressures of the process. During that process, whether you're male or female, you really have to pick which battles you want to fight. If you're out there to make a film, it's best to concentrate on getting the film made.

L) I think this carries over to other areas of management. Because you're a producer or director, you're really a manager, an administrator, as well as a creative person.

K) Right.

L) But you sometimes have to assert that it will be your vision that's going to prevail. I've had similar experiences. I've never produced or directed. . . . I have actually produced and directed films, small audio-visual presentations, but it's more in running my department, the Film and Media Department, that I run into this, too. If I say, shut up, I know what I'm doing, and I'll make these decisions, people do exactly what you said. So you have to be more diplomatic than a male in a comparable situation.

K) That's true.

L) Your film *First Look* is about Cuban painters. How much time have you spent in Cuba?

K) I had the unusual opportunity to spend ten months in Cuba in 1980, as the editor of a United States produced documentary about the Caribbean island of Grenada under the prime ministership of Maurice Bishop.

I lived in Havana, worked at ICAIC, the Cuban film institute, which houses all the film production facilities there.

L) Are the facilities good?

K) A lot of the equipment there originally came from the United States, so the facilities are in some ways comparable. Of course, the equipment is often old and not the most up-to-date technology. The rupture of trade relations between the United States and Cuba makes servicing, obtaining replacement parts, updating that equipment very difficult, if not impossible.

For us, the main problem was that most of the Cuban film industry works in 35mm, and this film, like most documentaries from here, was in 16mm.

L) So what happens? The movieola or whatever you needed was the wrong size?

K) No, they have a few 16mm editing machines, but if that's not the normal format used by the institution, there will be fewer machines, fewer pieces of peripheral equipment, the lab time is longer, the quality of the lab work goes down. In the final soundmix, it came as a total surprise to me that we couldn't really stop and start at different portions of the film with any ease. The old mixing consoles just didn't allow that.

L) What did you think of life in Cuba?

K) I was thrilled with the chance to spend time there. Friends say I'll go to any length to escape New York winters, but it was a tremendous opportunity to be able to stay there for so long and to work within my profession. I tend to be leery of two-week delegations who are jetted off to international "hot spots" to exchange preconceived thoughts in a largely symbolic gesture of friendship. Ten months, especially ten working months, afforded me a close look at Cuba, its mixture of Latin-Caribbean socialist culture.

L) Did you like it?

K) If you mean that in the same sense one might ask about any country, say, do you like France or Italy, of course I liked it. How could you dislike a country or people?

In the case of Cuba, the "do you like" question is usually a loaded one. In the United States, it's often not even a rationally thought out question and can even mean do you support Cuba, right or wrong? I'm assuming that's not what you mean.

L) How did you start in editing?

K) I started years ago in a documentary film production company in Paris, where I did an apprenticeship in editing (and learned French). I already knew then that I wanted to edit films and then direct my own films.

That was in 1973, after I graduated from college. Knowing that I wanted to travel and to work in films, with those vague plans in mind, I took off and I was very lucky.

We had just come out of the 60s—the civil rights movement, the antiwar movement, the women's movement. A lot of people took years off from college or spent some years after college traveling. It was like a generation of students taking a deep breath—very different from today when college graduates seem more short of breath as they rush off to business or law school.

L) Did you study film as an undergraduate?

K) No, I studied English literature at Harvard University.

L) Did they offer film at Harvard when you were there?

K) They have a Visual Studies Department, which is an amalgam of film, photography, and painting, I think. There's no such thing as a film major. Also, I chose not to study film.

L) Did you have the chance to do anything with it in high school, or did you just think about it?

K) I thought about it. I already knew my interests were in that direction. I even wrote some amateurish film reviews and tried my hand at theater. But my decision to study literature at Harvard didn't come out of the lack of a film department there. I felt that it was the one chance to sit back and read books for a few years. And I didn't want a training just in F-stops. I think the "classroom" principles of film are simple. The complexities only become apparent as you make films, in dealing with the problems that come up, or in dealing with the specific situations. Certainly it helps to know your apertures and shooting ratios, but that you can learn. What happens if you've mastered all that and then have nothing to say?

L) Was Radcliffe feminist during the time you were there?

K) Radcliffe College at Harvard has always had a strong tradition of being a women's institution. Even today, I get mail from them that focuses on women's concerns. The Radcliffe experience certainly would indicate that your environment determines your attitudes. You come out of there unaware of many of the more obvious constraints on women.

L) Even in the 50s when I was at Barnard, I didn't think of it as being feminist, but they just kept telling me, you can do anything you want to do. You can be the president, you can be a doctor, and can at the same time get married and have children. Just do anything because we've done it. That's how it was. You get the crazy idea that it's true.

K) And then you find out whether it can be true.

As I said, I wanted to go to Paris, to live in Paris. Maybe I read too much Balzac or had seen too many Godard and Truffaut films, but I wanted to live in Paris, and I wanted to work in films.

In retrospect, there were obviously a number of handicaps. One, I didn't speak French, except for a few recurrent phrases in Godard films. Two, I had no hands-on experience in film, I had no skills to offer anyone.

So I was lucky to meet some people who had just come back from a documentary shoot in Brazil. They invited me to work with them as an apprentice editor.

L) What exactly did you do?

K) At first, I had to figure out what people were talking about. Gradually it became easier because certain things are obvious. If you're handed a roll of film that's tails out, it becomes pretty obvious that whatever they're saying, they must be telling you to make it heads out. Eventually you learn to put the word together with the action.

L) So you pretty much learned French while on the job.

K) Yes. They were very patient with me, of course. I also learned the mechanics of editing. It was very basic training, but it's absolutely crucial.

L) How to make a clean splice.

K) Yes.

L) You weren't studying Eisensteinian montage at that point?

K) No. It was a question of how to wind from one end of the rewind to the other, how to use the splicer, how to find a trim in the bin. I loved it.

L) Did you get an editing credit on any of the films that you worked on for them?

K) You know, I don't even remember. I was so happy to be splicing, and then, just so happy to be splicing and knowing how to say it in French. I didn't have a really clear concept of credits or their importance. I was learning skills and making contacts. Everything else came much later.

L) How long have you been in New York?

K) For about ten or eleven years. I went briefly to film school, but left when I found editing work in the summer after my first year. Having had the Paris work experience, I knew how much more I could gain from learning on the job with pay, rather than at my expense in the classroom.

L) What projects have you worked on?

K) Everything from Robert Richter's independently produced documentary *Vietnam: An American Journey* and WGBH-TV's *Nova* series to Mike Nichols's *Gilda Live* and commercials for dog food, toilet paper, headache tablets. All of those projects have proved helpful experience to me in producing and directing now.

L) It seems that when you're making a film, not only do you do all the things that you have to do when you're directing in the theater, working with the talent, working with the lights, all the technical aspects, but you also have another layer of everything else. It seems that it's double. With the theater, you have much more preproduction perhaps, but with film you have more postproduction.

K) That's actually not true. Preproduction is really key to filmmaking, to know what you're looking for.

L) But do you rehearse it?

K) If it's a dramatic film, you do. In a documentary, you call it research. You have to talk to all the people you want in your film, plan it out, find out what their concerns are so that in the end, people say things that are true to themselves, but which also fit into the film you're making.

L) That's interesting about documentary directors really shaping as much as "dramatic" or feature directors. Other people I've talked to, and certainly other people I've read about, said that. The public's naive illusion that they're seeing a piece of reality as it really, really is, is nonsense, because you've shaped it.

K) Sure. You wouldn't bother being a filmmaker if you couldn't shape it. It's a kind of rehearsal process in preproduction. There's talking, preparation, finding out who the people are, and what they have to say. Also, preproduction in documentary films is important because these people are not actors and actresses. Imagine someone in a documentary. He or she is suddenly sitting in a room with all these lights on them, and all these people running around, and has to feel confidence in the person talking to them, directing them. That comes from talking or spending time together beforehand—just like in dramatic films, actors and actresses develop a relationship with the director during rehearsals.

L) If you're deliberately shaping events as a filmmaker, you sometimes get criticized. Sometimes if the technique is obvious, it's more honest. On the other hand, if your documentary is so subtle that no one notices, it's less honest because you're really there anyway. And you are a factor, you are a participant in the event, but people respect your seamless approach to it. It seems very ironic. Is it easier to work in feature films without that hypocrisy of pretending that you're not there when you're really there?

K) It's true. You can't be invisible. But I think people get stuck on that point, too. No film is reality. It's always someone's version of reality, their perception of reality. All film is, in your words, "pretending."

But it *is* very difficult to deal with real people on the production level when it comes to scheduling or having things happen when you want them to happen. Everything is more difficult. It's so much easier just to block out this house and say we're shooting a dramatic film here and know that somebody's baby is not going to cry in the next room. Also, actors know what they're supposed to say and do. On the other hand, documentaries have a freshness, a spontaneity that only real people can bring to film.

L) Well, to the issue of control, which is every artist's issue. It's an interplay between control and giving up control, seeing what happens and capturing something that can happen spontaneously, which is worth holding onto. You have an opportunity to fix things in a sense, a bit more afterwards.

K) In terms of editing?

L) Compared to work in the theater.

K) Oh, sure, the live moment is not it. You can deal with some things later, that's true. But it's also very dangerous to go shoot a film saying, I'll fix it later because what you have is what you have. There's a joke among production people when things are going badly, people start saying to one another, "We'll fix it in the mix." But that's the wry humor of a hopeless situation.

Some directors do a lot of actual filmmaking.

They edit for a while, then they film hundreds of thousands of feet more in search of their story. But there's a point when you have to stop collecting, and you must work with the material.

It also goes back to what you were saying about control. People in mental hospitals draw pictures, right? For that matter, anyone can draw a picture, right? The difference between these drawings, which may be perfectly beautiful, and those considered the professional work of painters is control. The same thing applies to films. You can go around collecting images ad infinitum, but the difference between a random collector of images and a filmmaker is control, and a vision of not just the parts, but the sum of the parts, the whole.

L) Tell me about your film *First Look.*

K) *First Look* is a documentary about painters who've grown up with the Cuban Revolution and the visit of two of these artists to the United States in the first cultural exchange of its kind since the Cuban Revolution.

The idea came out of my ten-month stay in Cuba. I was struck by the diversity of artwork there. When I heard Choco Roca and Nelson Dominguez had been invited to exhibit their work in the United States, the idea for the film became clearer. After all, my stay there had really taught me the value of cultural exchange.

In August 1981 we went to Cuba for a week with nine rolls of film that a friend had given me, a few thousand dollars that someone else contributed, and a Master Charge card. We shot very little, nine rolls is not much, but enough to put together a showreel to raise more money and get the film off the ground.

L) Who was on your team? Who was part of the crew?

K) I went down with Veronica Selver who codirected and recorded sound, and Burleigh Wartes, who was the cameraperson at that point. Later, when Burleigh had a schedule conflict, Don Lenzer finished the filming. Both of them did a terrrific job.

L) Did you own your own cameras and sound equipment?

K) No, a lot of people who worked on the film, people with a lot of experience and a lot of talent who agreed to work on it for very little money, brought their own equipment and gave a lot to the film.

And considering that actual production time takes up so small a portion of the calendar year, it really doesn't make sense for us to have our own equipment.

L) Working with the lab, that's something you learned a lot about when you are doing editing. You know just what to expect and demand. I guess it's a kind of negotiation. Did you get a print, a final print, that you're pleased with?

K) I work with DuArt, and I must say I'm very satisfied with the technical quality of their work. If it weren't for their concern for their clients, the print that you saw wouldn't have gotten out that day. It came out at nine o'clock in the morning.

I picked it up, jumped into a car, and got it over to your screening.

L) It seems to me lurking in the back of your mind was always the notion you would be a film-maker, but not a sense of I'm going to become a filmmaker to the exclusion of all else. Sometimes when I ask women who are painters, or in the visual arts, "When did you decide to become an artist?" they say, "Well, I always knew," but I don't think it's quite clear with you, that you always knew since childhood. You evolved toward it. Is that an accurate feeling? Or did you always know?

K) I've known very clearly for a long time that I would be making films someday, but I never felt I had to run out and make films to prove it. So the evolution you sense has not been one of goals, but rather the process of reaching that goal, of mixing in varying proportions from moment to moment, all the elements that go into a film.

Part of my attraction to films is that in being a filmmaker one doesn't exclude all else. Film is closely wedded to painting, literature, music, history, sociology and it's always about people.

L) Did you have a specific background in art for making *First Look*?

K) Not an academic background but a life-long interest in it, perhaps planted by one of my favorite uncles, a very talented painter who died young.

I'd like to see more attention given to the art of nonAmerican, nonEuropean, nonmasters. In *First Look*, the Cuban painter Wilfredo Lam says, "Our culture nourishes the culture of Europe. But the heritage of the Third World is never recognized as an equal. Europe still sees it as a colony. In my paintings I want the two cultures to meet as equals." I agree with Lam.

I would also agree with those who think a lot of the value attached to "museum class" artists had less to do with honoring their work than with increasing the bank accounts of art investors. The resulting mystification of art has been catastrophic for the artist and the art audience. People worry that they might not like the "right" painting, or they may not understand the style and language of art. Most people don't even look at art. But then, most people don't matter to highbrows of the art world.

It would probably be more honest to take the paintings out of the museums and leave up only the labels with the artists' names. That's what most people have been browbeaten into spending more time on any way, not enjoying art.

L) Who are your favorite directors or people that have had an influence on your style?

K) Whether they've had a visible influence on my style or not, I'd hesitate to say, but there are certainly people whose work I admire. For my generation, film was what literature had been to an earlier generation. We grew up with a seemingly odd mixture of Humphrey Bogart and Jean-Luc Godard and François Truffaut. Some of the Indian filmmakers—Mrinal Sen and Satyajit Ray—I like their work very much. Then there's Fellini's *Amarcord*, Woody Allen's *Annie Hall.*

It would be hard to say there's one person who's influenced me but I've seen many, many films, and I know that lots of films are floating around inside me.

L) Are there women who've served as "role models" for you?

K) Not really. Women directors are still too few and far between for that. And we haven't started to see ourselves in that way.
That's something we have to learn from men, who benefit a great deal from their mentors.

L) The people you mentioned as influences are feature filmmakers who have had some commercial success. It's been my observation that a lot of women work in documentary partly because they have something that they want to say that is expressible through that format, but partly also because other avenues are closed off to them. Do you want to become a feature filmmaker or commercial—whatever that means—filmmaker, or are you planning to stay with documentaries?

K) I'm interested in making dramatic films. I don't think that anybody who decided as a child or as a young girl to become a filmmaker could have been thinking in documentary terms directly because your decisions are usually based on what you see around you. How many documentaries had I seen at that point? Not very many.
But more than anything, I dislike this need for categorization, for setting up false oppositions. Five years from now I may make a dramatic film. Ten years from now I may make a documentary. All films tell a story. The idea dictates the format.

L) Yes. Your film *First Look* was hard to categorize. People kept saying, well, it should be in the art category, we don't know if it's international affairs—

it's really not—and people kept saying, well, but it's political, you know; it was an interesting discussion that we had.

K) Well, in that film it's that combination that interests me. Art and politics, the meeting of individual artists and cultures.

Films have to distill a lot of material for the audience, but they shouldn't oversimplify, reduce everything to its lowest common denominator. Politicians do enough of that.

L) You're distributing your own film?

K) No, Icarus Films is distributing it. We don't have the time or the capital to go into the distribution business, which is something in itself. Anyway, Icarus has an extensive library of Latin American/Caribbean films and a broad outreach to that audience.

We also have a special arrangement for distribution through the American Federation of Arts, so the film can reach the art audience as well.

L) And *First Look* has been shown on television?

K) Yes, on PBS.

L) Is that a major outlet for independent films?

K) It's the single largest audience for most independent films. But independent producers need to look elsewhere for real distribution.

PBS's greatest crime is its financial mistreatment of independent producers. But an even more fundamental problem and PBS's greatest misfortune has been its inability to nurture an independent artistic vision. Rather than working closely with American independents, PBS has chosen to take an adversarial role, which in the end, probably reflects the state of our society as a whole. But in its failure to encourage creativity, artistic daring, and freshness, PBS itself is the loser. It has become the woefully backward cousin of similarly mandated and far more successful television networks in other countries.

L) Now, one of your business names is the production company.

K) Riverfilms is the name of my company. My name "Kavery" is the name of a river in India. I'm drawn to water as a strong source image anyway and, of course, rivers are the source of civilization.

L) You had a grant for *First Look*?

K) *First Look* was funded by a number of sources—from the New York Council for the Humanities and the New York State Council on the Arts to the Film Fund, Beard's Fund, the National Council of Churches, the Playboy Foundation, to name a few. We were very successful in putting together a financial patchwork by appealing to a wide range of funding priorities—art, Latin America, and the Caribbean cultural exchange.

L) Was it difficult getting the money together?

K) Finding the money is always difficult for profit *and* nonprofit films, documentary *and* dramatic films.

The nonprofit route makes it possible to make

films whose value can't be measured by box-office success. It's also an avenue open to producers and directors who may have less or no access to commerical opportunities.

But the grant world poses its own problems for the independent producers. Many months are lost in a bureaucratic decision-making process that will yield only one fraction of your total budget.

I also find it peculiar that final funding decisions are made by committees/panels/boards that never meet face to face with the filmmaker. That system may be the key to the basic concept of bureaucracy, but it doesn't lend itself to arts funding where much of the decision has to depend on one's assessment of the capabilities of those with fiscal and creative responsibility.

L) Do you think funding gets easier with each successive project?

K) Not in the case of the grant world today. I see the situation worsening for everyone as funding dries up. The money is still out there but filmmakers' access to it will become increasingly limited.

Part of that problem is a situation which we as filmmakers have passively accepted. Still today, most film funding comes through the bending/distorting/compromising of a project to fit the scholarly, political, or community priorities of funding organizations. Our success lies in getting these institutions to award money to films, but it's never in film terms. So underlying the whole process is the usual insecurity of any illegitimate child. Films will be at the top of the list of organizational budget cuts we already see coming our way.

L) How did you get Harry Belafonte?

K) I knew he'd been to Cuba, he's even performed there. In fact, the year I was editing in Havana, in the room next to mine, a Cuban editor was working on a documentary filmed with Harry on one of his visits to Cuba.
I had approached him when we were organizing a fundraiser for the film. He was very supportive of the project and spoke on its behalf at the fundraiser. Later, I was eager to have a narrator who knew something about Cuba and whose style of delivery would also lend itself to a less formal narration presence. And that was Harry.

L) Do you consider yourself a feminist?

K) Strictly a feminist, no, I don't. Perhaps because the word "feminist" here is associated mostly with white American women. I believe in women's rights. I support ERA. But in the United States, feminist concerns are very limited to issues of sex, so the overwhelming majority of active feminists are white middle-class women. I myself am not only a woman but also an Asian-American of Indian origin. I share the concerns of American feminists but find their vision limited. You can't isolate issues of sex from issues of race or class.

L) Do you think you have to make a choice between sex and race?

K) I don't think you do. In the same way that I don't think *First Look* has to be strictly about art or about politics, I don't think one has to be simply a feminist or "Third-Worldist" or environmentalist or disarmamentist.

Although I support the goals of the feminist movement, I think that movement needs to make much more active overtures to nonwhite women. The concerns of white middle-class American women are very different from those of people of nonwhite or nonmiddle-class origin. The American feminist needs to recognize that and realize that in the end, the movement can only go so far without the active support of all of us.

L) Do women's issues concern you as a filmmaker?

K) I bring to my films a strong awareness of women's issues which I deal with in the context of the film as a whole.

As a filmmaker, I find all too often an overwhelming preoccupation among "feminists" with the mere pumping out of images of women. I don't have all the answers, but I'm not so sure that just because a film has many women in it and is made by a woman, it can be called a women's film without any consideration of content or point of view. Nor am I so sure that films about women merrily murdering men (and I mean merrily) reflect any meaningful approach to women's issues.

L) I'm very torn between the issues that are specific to women cross-culturally in the arts and some of the issues that you raise, the things that are unique to each culture or factors that are characterized more by class, race, or social structure, regardless of where you live. It is a complex issue; and I'm also very wary of politics. I get very nervous about politics in the arts and in film but also aware that it's there. The film world is political in itself, and then there's the bigger issue of the big politics or international politics.

K) I'm very much for dialogue with all women. I don't think if it's a closed door, that it should stay closed. I just think that aspect hasn't really been explored, or been given a priority.

L) It's interesting in *First Look*, in the parts done in Cuba, that the men, it seemed to me (and I don't know if you did this consciously or if was an accident), the two artists who are certainly wonderful and warm and interesting, were not particularly concerned about women's issues. When they came to California and met with the San Francisco artists, they suddenly seem to have had their consciousness raised about women artists. Maybe there was a shift in their perception of the role of women in art today. It seemed a new aspect, a new dimension of the political situation, too. I don't know what it's like now for women artists in Cuba. I was relieved that you did show some of the work of women artists in Cuba. But it didn't seem to be an issue for the two men until they got to the United States.

K) That's true. After all, Cuba subscribes to the macho culture of Latin America. Choco, in being here, did learn a lot about women, women professionals, how they should be treated, what their problems were, what their concerns were, which is why, when he goes back, he does talk about it at the press conference. He was struck by this, and told me a number of times that women here are very "strong" and "different." I think what he sensed was that women here demanded to be treated a certain way.

L) So, what goes on with women artists in

Cuba? Do you think they're getting their fair shake in the artists' community? Are they treated as equals?

K) In terms of legislation, yes. Cuba even has laws that guarantee equal pay for women. In terms of reality, however, the day-to-day problems of women lie in cultural limitations that will take generations to change. I see a change already between the older generation and the younger one. The younger ones being the people in their 30s now. But, still, it'll take a few more generations to change that, to change the world of women there. Have you seen *Lucia*? Humberto Solas's film *Lucia* is very telling of the changes that are happening, the changes that have yet to happen. But I don't think that a macho culture like that can change so quickly. (Our own culture hasn't either.) In Cuba many of the women told me that they see a difference in their children, too. Their children of five or six. And that's where one's hope must lie.

L) Did you meet many Cuban women filmmakers and filmworkers?

K) Sure. I met many editors. There aren't many women directors, just one at this point who directs documentaries. Certainly no camerapeople or sound recordists. But I know a number of Cuban women who want a chance to direct. They're politely knocking at the door now. And the door will have to open very soon.

To us living here, it may look like they're slow. They should be beating down those doors, but they know what works in their context. And I'm certain they'll succeed.

L) What are you working on now?

K) I'm making a film about calypso music. We've filmed in Trinidad, the Caribbean birthplace of calypso, and in Brooklyn. Most people don't realize Brooklyn is the big center for recording calypso.

It's great music, with witty lyrics and often sharp commentary. The calypsonians themselves are a lively bunch of people to work with. We've filmed with Kitchener, Rose, Duke, really the calypso greats, following them all the way to Trinidad Carnival, where the calypso monarch of the year is selected.

Incidentally, Calypso Rose is the first woman to become a success in the traditionally male calypso world. She talks about that in the film.

L) What stage are you in?

K) Postproduction. We're not too far from completion.

Filmgoers are always surprised to find out how long it takes to make a film, from the idea to the launching of the project to its completion. That's why it's important to make films you can live with for a while.

CHRONOLOGY

One Hand Don't Clap	Upcoming release
Soul Gone Home	1985
First Look	1983
Americas in Transition	No date
The Real Thing	No date
A Plague on Our Children	No date
Gilda Live	No date

TAMI GOLD

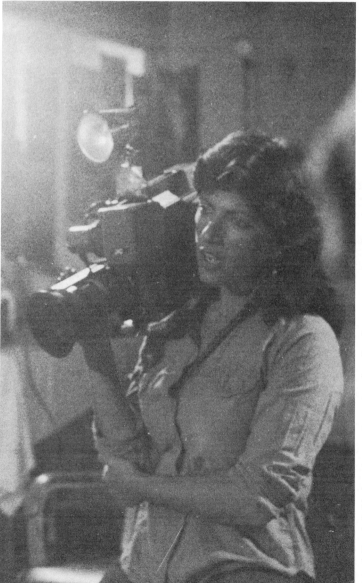

Tami Gold shooting an interview for the documentary, *Looking for Love: Teenage Parents.*
Photo credit: Christine Vogel.

Tami Gold was born in New York City. She has two daughters, Amilca Palmer, born in 1975, and Shannon Ahern, born in 1982, and lives in Jersey City, New Jersey.

Gold attended Friends World College (1970) and the University of Havana, and studied extensively in Mexico and other Latin American countries. She is a member of the Association of Independent Video and Filmmakers, the New Jersey Media Artists Network, Media Alliance, and Media Network.

She is a producer/director of numerous works that have been shown on network television, cablevision, and the Public Broadcasting System.

Her documentaries have been funded by The Film Fund, the New Jersey State Council on the Arts, the Labor Institute for Public Affairs, Mid-Atlantic Regional Fellowship, Essex County Community Development Grant, The Victoria Foundation, The Prudential Foundation, Legal Services Corporation, The Center for New Television, and others.

Her work has received numerous awards at many festivals, including the American Film Festival; the Athens Video Festival; Leipzig Film Festival, East Germany; Women in the Director's Chair, Chicago, 1985 and 1987; the 1984 New Jersey Video and Film Festival; the 1985 National Housing Media Festival; Chicago International Film and Video Festival; The United States Film and Video Festival; The Global Village Video Festival; The Sony National Video Festival; Black Maria Film and Video Festival; and the Flaherty Documentary Festival.

Gold is the director of New Jersey's Annual Video and Film Festival; a professor of Documentary and Video Production at New York University's Tisch School of the Arts; and the director of Media Programming at Media Works in Newark. She was the director and coordinator of the National Video Festival and coordinator and instructor of video workshops for Downtown Community Television Center.

She has received fellowships from The John Simon Guggenheim Memorial Fellowship-Video Artist; the New Jersey State Council on Arts, Video Artist; and the Mid-Atlantic Regional Arts Fellowship.

She has lectured and exhibited her work at the following institutions: Film in the City, Yale University; University of Connecticut; Columbia University; Adelphi University; Hunter College; The Newark (N.J.) Museum; The Old State House, Hartford, Connecticut; The New York Film Council; The Kennedy Center (AFI): The Film Fund; Women Make Movies; The Foundation for Independent Video and Film, Inc.; University Community Video Center, Minneapolis; St. Paul Public Access Center, Minnesota; and Fairfield University.

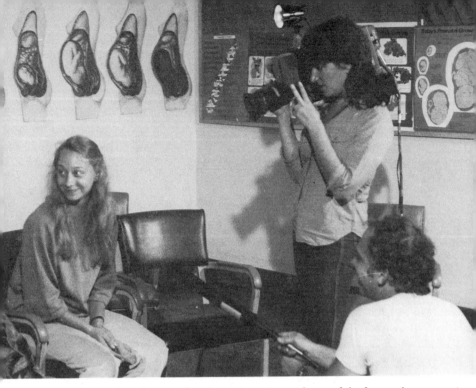

Tami Gold with Erik Lewis shooting an interview with one of the featured teenagers in the documentary, *Looking for Love: Teenage Parents*. Photo credit: Christine Vogel.

Tami Gold teaching a video editing class at New York University.

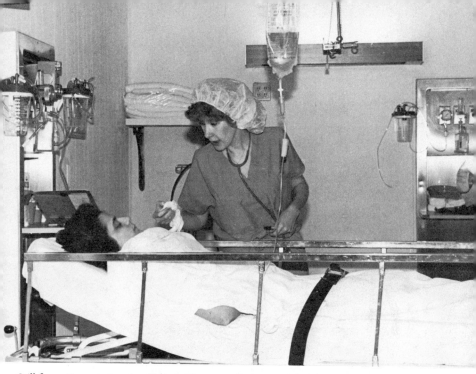

Still from *Prescription for Change*. Photo credit: Lyn Goldfarb.

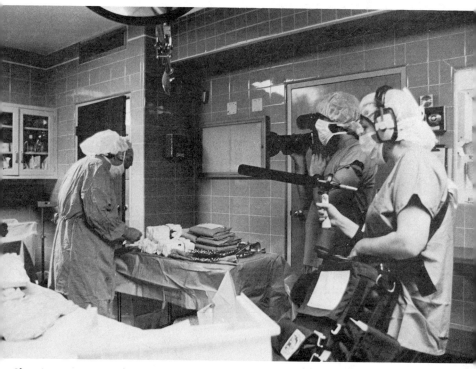

Shooting *Prescription for Change*. Photo credit: Lyn Goldfarb.

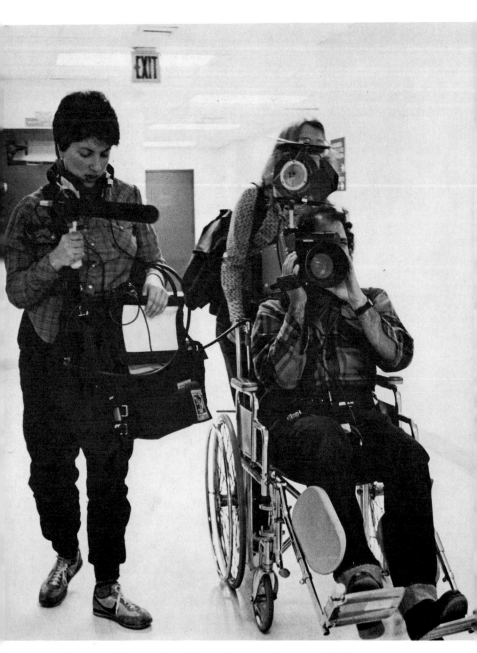

Shooting *Prescription for Change*. Photo credit: Lyn Goldfarb.

INTERVIEW

Interview on September 23, 1985, with Tami Gold, the producer and director of *From Bedside to Bargaining Table, Looking for Love, Signed, Sealed and Delivered,* and *Prescription for Change.*

L) Tell me about how and why you started in television and film.

T) I went to Friends World College, a Quaker school founded on the belief that the way to have world peace was for people to be educated interculturally. The school sent me to South America. I also spent many years in South America outside the school. I was an artist. Many of the paintings in the house are mine.

L) That past in art interests me very much because that's where my interest in film comes from, too. I had coordinated the Women Artists Series at Douglass and worked with many artists over the years, so I'm excited about that connection to art.

T) I went to Mexico and studied mural painting with Señor Salze, who was a student of Diego Rivera. He was never considered a great painter but a good muralist. I studied with him for a year. I was very much interested in the integration of art and politics, which is so prevalent in South America and especially in Mexico. I did an enormous amount of photography. I left Mexico in 1968. I received an art scholarship at the University of Havana. I went to Cuba to study painting. I was eighteen at the time. I didn't have the discipline necessary to stay put in Havana. I didn't study painting in

111

Cuba. I worked the harvest. I participated in the "10,000 tons of sugar cane" attempt to cut the sugar cane. I traveled all over the country and got close to filmmakers in Cuba. I always felt integrated into the Cuban art circle, but I also felt the need to know what was happening in all aspects of the country.

L) There is an institute for filmmaking in Cuba. Did you go there?

T) I didn't study film, but I was close to some of the filmmakers. There is a filmmaker in Cuba, Santiago Alvarez, who is famous for his experimental documentaries and minidocumentaries. I was introduced to him and others and as a result I learned about producing media for the masses. I left Cuba and went all through South America—hitchhiking, photographing, and writing—with two friends. When we got back to the United States, Heather Archibald and I showed friends our photographs and writings and someone said, "Why don't you go to the Rabinowitz Foundation? They might be interested." We went there and they said, "We really like your work. Why don't you go back down and make a film?" And they gave us $2,000. At that time, $2,000 was a lot more than it is now.

L) Even so, it wasn't a lot.

T) Yes, a miniscule amount of money. At 19 years of age, Heather and I returned to Central America, where we shot the film, *My Country Occupied.* We shot the whole film in black-and-white 16mm. It focuses on an Indian woman. It's about her life. It takes the personal story of one Indian woman and makes a general statement about U.S. imperialism. When we returned to New York after shooting the footage, not knowing anything about video or film, we got together with a group called Newsreel and became a part of the Newsreel collective in the early 1970s. I stayed with Newsreel for about three years, making and distributing films.

L) Did you learn editing?

T) Yes, at Newsreel they nursed us through the whole process of making a film. It was very gruelling. We made the film on very little money, and it's somewhat crude. I always thought that *My Country Occupied* was like a painting. It's like a montage, a painting, or a collage. It has visual impressions of people, women, and the tremendous impact that I felt the role my government had in Guatemala. It's all about Guatemala.

L) Is the film still around?

T) Yes, I have copies of the film.

L) Sounds like it means even more right now.

T) Sure, and the film actually had done very well in terms of distribution. It is a Newsreel film. It's in their catalog.

L) So Newsreel is still distributing *My Country Occupied?*

T) Yes. Although it's a very crude film, I think it's a good one because it's raw and to the point.

L) You had that youthful stance of "I'll try anything." You just went in there and did it. You didn't think about all the problems that you later knew too much about. You might never have done it if you had.

T) After being in Newsreel for a few years and doing many of the antiwar films and distribution, I left the media. I got a job at the Maxwell House Coffee Company in Hoboken. I wanted to work in heavy industry and did that for a while. I also got very involved with painting again and did painting primarily and secondarily, for a few years' photography. Eventually, I became a pipe fitter for Public Service Electric and Gas. I felt I really needed to do work that was nontraditional for women. When I was doing it, the conflict of not being an artist and of feeling totally isolated and alienated in the work became pretty drastic; I quit the job.

L) You say that when you were in the job as a pipe fitter, somehow you couldn't be an artist as well? It was a conflict of roles?

T) I felt I couldn't work those eight hours a day and then do my art. My oldest child was three years old then. Many people can do their painting on weekends and in the evenings; it wasn't enough time for me.

L) They fit it in around the edges.

T) I wasn't able to do that. I resented that conflict, and it put me at odds in jobs. I was always feeling very rebellious. I decided that I had to do something about it. I couldn't continue. I also felt painting wasn't enough for me because painting is a very isolated art form. It doesn't reach many people; it hangs in an individual's home. I couldn't make strong enough statements. I found it confining, and people wouldn't pay for it. You have to give it away or barter your work.

L) Or sell it to an institution.

T) Exactly. And then the conflict was, unless I were to end up like a Diego Rivera—doing that kind of public art, which is so very unlikely in the United States, making big statements in public art—I didn't want to paint. Our culture focuses on individual art, the individual painting. I just became very frustrated with it; I was fighting with every painting. I wasn't painting; I was fighting every canvas. I decided that I had to go back to film or do video.

L) Is television the American equivalent of the mural?

T) Yes, in its ability to reach many people.

L) What do you think is going on that we don't have a major public art form? Even television is very elitist when it comes to the major distribution channels, unless you're in alternative distribution. It's very controlled, even cable. How can people get access?

T) I think that we are a very practical people. We have had a particular kind of industrial revolution in this country. If art gets in the way of progress, we get rid of art. In Philadelphia they have whitewashed some of Diego Rivera's murals because they needed the walls for other things. This is criminal.

L) It's like whitewashing "The Last Supper" or the Sistine Chapel ceilings.

T) We don't take art seriously when teaching

our children. Art is always extracurricular in most schools. In the inner city schools, they never even get to it. It's something that people can have for their children only on the weekends. It's a select few who go to music school, who have exposure to painting, dance, and theater. I am an artist and a social activist. It's very hard to integrate the two. It has been a constant battle. It was a battle in my high school. In fact, I did many sculptures in high school. There are a few sitting around my house. I actually was expelled from a school because the authorities didn't find some of the sculptures palatable. I made sculptures of women loving each other.

L) Summarizing so far, it sounds to me as if you always wanted to work in the arts, even when you were very young, but that for you the arts were connected with your social concerns, which have always been there, too. And then television came in much later as a result of your making a definite decision to get into a mass culture medium. But how did you know in the first place that you wanted to be an artist? Is it something that you were just born knowing or did your parents help you with that?

T) I think that it was always there. My mother cultivated it, allowed that to be.

L) Were your parents in the arts?

T) No, my parents were very attracted to the arts. My father was a factory worker and, when I was a child, my mother worked as a saleswoman periodically, until I was around ten. When I was ten, she went back to school and got a high school diploma, eventually received a B.A., and then went on to get

her M.S.W. Now she's a therapist. My mother encouraged me to create since I was a child. My father
was more passive; he didn't understand it. I quit high
school at a very young age. I was not a "good student." Eventually, after a lot of turmoil and disap-
pointment, I received a high school diploma. It was a
hard thing, but I got the diploma. Then I was able to
go to Friends World College, a Quaker college.

L) Did you major in art at the college?

T) Always, and I don't really think it was a
matter of making a decision. It was always something that I was attracted to.

L) I always wonder about where the art impulse comes from because so many people say it just
WAS. They say, "My parents didn't teach me. My
mother wasn't an artist, my father wasn't an artist."
I'm always curious about where art comes from.

T) I don't know where it comes from, because there wasn't really that much around me in
suburban Levittown.

L) Did you go to films as a child?

T) The first film I ever went to see was
Oklahoma, and that was very rare. We were not
allowed much television, and there were very few
books in our home.

L) Magazines? Newspapers?

T) Very little. My parents were not intellec-
tuals.

L) When did you begin working with Newark
MediaWorks?

T) I got started with video before I became involved with Newark MediaWorks. I did a documentary called *Signed, Sealed and Delivered,* about the Jersey City post office and the struggle that went on there over the issue of workers' health and safety and the question of the right to strike, which many, many organized workers don't have, and that unorganized workers certainly don't have. I am very interested in labor issues. This was another crudely produced documentary that won awards and wide recognition. It's very much from the perspective of the rank and file, not from that of the union leaders or management.

L) The person, the worker. It was shown at the American Film Festival in New York and won an award there.

T) It also won some top awards in international festivals, as well as cash awards; it was shown on PBS and has had a big effect in the whole area of grass roots media. Through producing *Signed, Sealed and Delivered,* I reentered the media world.

After I produced this documentary, I became involved with Downtown Community TV Center in New York City, a really alternative, fabulous TV center. I received one of the C.E.T.A. art scholarships. They gave me an $18,000 salary to do media (for eighteen months). For me, it was a fantastic opportunity because it gave me a year and a half to totally, intensely get myself into what I believed and wanted to do. It was right before Reagan, and then, of course, Reagan slashed the whole C.E.T.A. program. I was still part of the C.E.T.A. arts program when Reagan was elected. When C.E.T.A. folded, Downtown Community TV hired me. I did a lot of community documentaries, taught classes, became involved with the idea that video could be a community expression, not just an individual artistic expression. I was the director of the first American Community TV Festival at Downtown Community TV Center. It was an absolute success. After three years of working at Downtown Community TV I felt somewhat frustrated. It's a funny thing with me, I continue to have to do my own work.

L) That's good. It would be too bad if you didn't.

T) I wasn't satisfied with doing the community video work, coordinating the festival, and supporting the big producers there.

L) Who were the producers?

T) Jon Alpert and Keiko Tsuno. I remain friendly with them, but felt that I needed my own production work in addition to coordinating and directing others'.

L) That's too administrative. It's good, but it's one remove from making, touching, work.

T) I took a leave of absence from DCTV but maintained a closeness. Then I started working on *Looking for Love*, about teenage pregnancy in Newark, East Orange, and other Essex County communities. I did that with Christine Vogel and Newark MediaWorks.

Looking for Love is an example of an effective documentary, yet was produced with approximately $8,000—community television. At that same time, I started work on another production on Northern Ireland called *The Last Hunger Strike*, for PBS.

L) I've seen a good deal of video and film. To me the factor that illuminates good realist work is the truth that you can connect with in people's lives. No matter how expensive the piece, if you don't have the integrity it's ineffective.

T) I agree.

L) Sounds like you are involved with social activism and the labor community more than strictly with media professionals.

T) Yes, Elena Gensler, for example, was an associate producer of the nurse's tape, *Bedside to Bargaining Table*, and she's a nurse.

L) You have two nursing tapes.

T) The other nursing tape, *Prescription for Change*, is a longer piece. We are editing it right now. It's more an overview of nursing. Has feminism influenced the militancy of nursing? Are unions a solution to the problems and crises in nursing? What are the frustrations that women feel as nurses? Is there a higher rate of divorce among nurses? *Prescription for Change* is about two women: one woman is white, young, and works in a small, rural, private hospital. The other nurse is a Filipino woman who works in a public hospital. The first nursing piece, *From Bedside to Bargaining Table*, was named by Elena Gensler; she also named *Signed, Sealed and Delivered*. I think Elena has named almost all the documentaries I've worked on.

L) She has a flair for that.

T) Three nurses, Elena Gensler, Joanie Glickman, and Sarah Forman, were the associate producers. We feel that the integration of registered nurses in the piece is what structured and tailored it and made it work so well.

L) The piece is used as an organizing tool; nurses take it to meetings.

T) To me, it's a very good example of "narrow-casting"; that's a term that I hope starts to be used more often. It's the opposite of broadcasting. Broadcast television is for the broadest and the most general audience. In many ways it doesn't deal with any of the particular needs of anyone. It's the broadcast model of TV that is often described as mediocre. "Narrow-casting" can be fascinating; the whole idea of making television work in a different way, in a much more interactive way, is the main thrust. If we had somebody here from Mars or another planet, that creature would think that the peoples of the earth worshipped neon furniture because we have such a passive relationship to this neon thing in our homes. When people talk to me about how dangerous television is, I understand. I really believe it is dangerous. But the way to make it become an active part and a good part of our lives is to have it become interactive and I think "narrow-casting" can do that.

L) And it's useful. It makes TV more like something that you can share with someone else rather than just sit there.

T) When we were first shooting the larger piece, *Prescription for Change*, we had a lot of response from people who were in nursing every day and from unions. They said, "What you're doing is good, but it's not going to work for us. We need something that will work. We can't deal with too many issues." You have to address the key thing, and the key thing is the question of the conditions nurses work under, the question of the corporatization of the health care industry, and the effect all this has on patients' care. Ultimately, the solution to this is organizing. I was resistant at first; I didn't think it was attractive enough to produce for one audience. I thought it was going to be so tailored that it wasn't going to have anything exciting in it.

L) What do you mean tailored?

T) It was going to be answering certain very fine points and wasn't going to be able to explore bigger issues. But as it worked out, and it was a learning process for me, too, it became clear that by doing it this way, we answered a very big need in nursing. The proof of that is that we sold over 400 copies of the tape in one year. It's going to be on television, WNYC-TV is going to premiere it. We decided to show it there rather than Channel 13. Channel 13 would have done it, but they would have just stuck it in at some ungodly hour and have done no promotion for it, whereas WNYC, Channel 31, will do a lot of promotion, will feature it at prime time, and will reach out to a nursing audience and a health-care worker audience. The key thing was for it to work for nurses and it's really worked for them because it's being used. If 400 copies have been sold, you realize it is being used actively all over the country. It really works. Many other unions are using it also.

L) It's used as a paradigm. I know it's being used in labor courses.

T) Schools have purchased it. Nursing schools have purchased it. It's a very good example of how television can be interactive; television can be designed to produce discussions among the viewers. Since it's only twenty minutes long, people still have, in the course of meeting time or classroom time or lunchtime, at least twenty minutes left over to discuss it. It was all these kinds of considerations that went into the particular way it was designed. Lyn Goldfarb co-produced and co-directed *From Bedside to Bargaining Table* and brought her years of labor experience to this production.

L) She's the one who made *With Babies and Banners*. How did you meet her?

T) At first I was working on the nurses' tape alone and somebody told her about it. Lyn called me up and said, "I'm very interested in this topic; I need this information." And I said, "Let's meet," and it just worked out well.

L) Goldfarb's *With Babies and Banners* was one of the earlier feminist labor history films. Do you find it hard to work with another director?

T) I work better with Lyn than with anyone else. I'd rather work with a woman, and Lyn and I agree politically.

L) How did you find out about the technology of video? Did you find out about it in school?

T) No, I am self-taught. With each production

I am able to keep up with the new technology—which changes rapidly. I have to know it, because as women, we're challenged technically all the time. When you meet people, the first thing they do is test you.

L) Can you work this machine? Can you handle it? Deciding to challenge your technical knowledge instead of getting to the substance of the work.

T) Exactly. My feeling has always been that I have to know the technology of video and film production. I have to know, so that I never feel that I'm on the defensive.

L) What seems clear to me in your work is that you have made a choice that the issues of the people are a priority, and that whether you spend $2,000 or $10,000, you're going to do the best you can with the issues and the people; the technology is the tool to capture the issues and the people's lives. But somehow with certain producers it gets twisted the other way around: the technology becomes the glamorous thing. That's the toy, that's what we want to play with, that's the fun thing.

T) That's definitely the quicksand that traps many people, once they get to TV. The sad thing is that it happens to many women.

L) And then they get disconnected from their content.

T) I've seen it happen to many, many women, many Afro-Americans. They lose the content. You'd think that they'd be taking their own experiences into it, but somehow it gets lost in the quicksand.

The nursing piece was a very highly produced piece. It had a high budget, different in that way from *Looking for Love*. Working on something like that was good for my own growth, technically, and I needed to take big steps forward in terms of budget size, and in terms of working with more state-of-the-art equipment. That was one consideration; the other consideration was who was going to use it. It's going to be used by nurses. Nurses are definitely a group of people who have a particular identity; they've been fed that identity: they are middle-class," they are "professionals." Somehow a grainier, community-oriented and low budgeted documentary might not have worked very well, structurally and stylistically. We worked with what I would consider a rather handsome budget on that piece.

L) Who funded it?

T) We received a grant from The Film Fund; we received a loan from the Center for New Television in Chicago; I received money from the New Jersey State Council of the Arts in the form of a fellowship. Then we received money from the unions; from LIPA (the AFL-CIO's Labor Institute for Public Affairs). We figured that that was a $50,000 piece. Of course, we did shooting for more than one production. A lot of footage is going into the longer piece. We were able to cut two stories for the news out of the same footage. It was a multiuse piece. I look at it as having a decent budget to work with for the kind of quality we wanted to get in the end.

L) What did more money enable you to do? Was it that you hired more crew?

T) No, just much better equipment.

L) Rented or purchased?

T) I wouldn't purchase it. I rented; I don't own the means of production—too expensive.

L) Is that a hassle?

T) I have friends who have equipment, and they make deals with me. It's a bit of a hassle. A group of friends and I started a small production house in New York City called 29th Street Video. We did that right after Reagan was elected. We were very concerned that independent producers, especially those doing socially oriented media, would find very few sources of financial support. We started a very small production company.

L) You have the editing decks there?

T) Sound mix and three-quarter-inch sound and editing. Very good, very good for industrial work. I've done a lot of work there; it's fine. But I couldn't do the nurses tape there.

L) Is it run as a co-op?

T) No, it's incorporated as a business.

L) So if someone who's not an owner wants to use it they have to pay a fee?

T) Yes. It became more of a business, and it didn't meet my needs. If it were more of a co-op, it would have met my needs more for rough-cut editing, before I went into a final editing stage. It didn't do that. So, basically, I had to buy my own equipment to do the rough cut of the nurses.

L) You have it here?

T) I had it where the desk is, there, in that room, under the bed. But I sold it, because it wasn't working out, doing all that work in the house. It just made whatever I did so much more the center of attraction than what anyone else did.

L) You didn't like that?

T) They didn't like it. I couldn't really see it at the time. Everybody didn't like it, from the youngest kid to the oldest adult. There were four kids and four adults at the time. That took a big toll. Ultimately, I sold the equipment and tried to make some changes and not have the intensity of the work I do dominate my living situation.

L) It's hard for an artist who is trying to integrate art-making with one's whole life; there's a tension there, whatever the medium is; it can be stained glass. I've known many artists, and the work just intrudes into their lives. A stained glass artist who is a friend of mine took over the living and dining rooms in her house. The house became almost all her work space and studio, because it had to be. What else could she do? The work was big and just took up more and more space; they recently had to move to a bigger house where she could have a separate studio. It becomes a matter of economics. You're trying to earn money to get more space.

T) I know. I decided at this point, having kids and having relatively small living quarters (this is pretty small), that I couldn't have it in the house, period. We were doing all the distribution. Can you imagine 400 video tapes being negotiated out of this space? It was really pretty crowded. It's just these two rooms and two rooms downstairs, that's it. The kitchen, and another room for the kids, and Elena has the two floors upstairs. That's all we have. Another thing has to do with the fact that everybody here does good work, a lot of work, and people don't want to feel that their work is second best. I don't have a comfortable working situation yet. I'm trying to get it together, to get something really comfortable, where I can do rough-cut editing before I go into my final edits, and a place I could work out of that I can afford. It's so expensive in New York City.

L) But you're as close as you can get. Jersey City really is very close, cuddled right up to New York.

T) Yes.

L) The personal issues interest me because even though I'm not an artist, I've been through some of the same things. The search for balance, needing to do your own work, and being alone and having your own life, and also needing the family, and the support and love and comfort that come with the closeness. There is constant tension.

T) There is a great deal of tension. So, I just cut down; I got a Guggenheim Fellowship, which is very nice, and I have started a new project. I'm doing a documentary on teenage unemployment, the whole issue of adolescence in the city, focusing on black and Hispanic youths, and taking a very hard look at the racism that has intensely penetrated the employment market.

L) Do you think it's worse now?

T) I think it's much worse. I think we have a situation where racism is accepted; white supremacy has always existed but, now, the openness of racism is more the norm. We have institutions that cut back phenomenally and feel justified by the Regan Administration. The effects of the Reagan Administration filter down into everything, even a YMCA or a women's shelter or the Job Corps. Consequently, we see cutbacks made all over. That word "cutback" is almost a cliché, but when you look inside the city, you see the real, human results of the word "cutback." Fifty percent of teenagers in New York City drop out of high school. Sixty percent of Hispanic youth in Newark are not and have never been enrolled in any public or private school system. They are not educated, not even to the third grade.

L) So for better or for worse, they're not touched by the great Americanizing machine that the schools have always been?

T) Yes, they will not be employable in any sense of the word. I think it's a time bomb.

L) You're going back to some of the issues that you dealt with in *Looking for Love*, picking up those strands.

T) Exactly. Initially, this project came from discussions that Christine Vogel and I had while producing *Looking for Love*. With *Looking for Love* the audience was the teenagers, primarily teenage girls. We wanted it to work for teenagers. And it does work for teenagers; it works very well. It also works well for other people. There's a real reaction to a pregnant minority teenager. When I received the Guggenheim Fellowship, I felt that this would be my chance to begin the documentary on teenage unemployment. I still have a lot to do. I'm finishing two minidocumentaries in Spanish about the housing crisis. I speak Spanish. We're doing that at Shelterforce. That's a lot to complete because I haven't even finished shooting it. Then, I have to finish the long nurses' piece, *Prescription for Change*, and I have another piece that I'm working on, which consists of material about my sister that I shot over a few years. I did some shooting of her prior to the diagnosis that her husband had cancer; eventually he died. I have some of that recorded on video.

L) About widowhood?

T) No, about their personal experience. I have all of the home movie film they took. I have the stills of when they were married, when she gave birth, and then the pain. While she was pregnant, my brother-in-law was diagnosed as having colitis. I have on video footage that I shot for Belleville Hospital on what it's like for adults in midlife to have a chronic illness—how does one adjust? It's a really interesting scene, because it's the interaction of my sister and her husband, and it's personal.

L) How old is your sister?

T) My sister is fifteen months older than I, and her husband died over two years ago. Two years ago in April. I've had all this footage for a very long time, and I haven't been able to edit it, but I do want to do that.

L) Tell me about feminism. Sounds to me as if you were born an artist, and might have been born a feminist, too, because you're strong. You have definite opinions. Did you run into any problems because you're a woman? Either as an artist or in film or television?

T) I really don't think so. First of all, I have a real advantage. I feel really blessed that I was a 60s kid. My parents belonged to the Communist Party and that was a big part of my life. I was raised with a strong sense of community; that was a very large part of my consciousness. When I was very vulnerable, very receptive, I was working at a place called World Fellowship. It's a religious and left wing place where, in the summer, people come together and share ideas. At age sixteen or seventeen, I met a woman who was in her late sixties and had a long history of involvement with social left politics. She had been part of the Lincoln Brigade in Spain, and she was with the underground.

L) Did you see that film by the way? *The Good Fight?*

T) Yes, beautiful, beautiful, beautiful film. I had the privilege to get very close to her, and she was an absolute feminist, before feminism was even an agenda item in the movement, in the 1960s.

L) It wasn't even part of the 60s movements. She was more from the 20s and 30s? That kind of feminism?

T) Yes, a lot of people said to me, "Oh, Sophie, she's stuck in the 30s; something's wrong with her." And I always knew nothing was wrong with her.

She was the person with whom I first celebrated International Woman's Day. She was fabulous, and I was very fortunate because I had the opportunity to stay with her a lot.

L) What kinds of things did she say?

T) She was brilliant. She would just talk, she was into women's issues and into the whole issue of black empowerment.

L) She saw that they're linked?

T) Of course, they're linked. Yes. She was married. Her husband was Afro-American, Joe Lillard, who was the first All Star football player but, of course, he was too early to have made it in sports. I got very close to her and Joe. She had cancer when I met her; she eventually died of it. I stayed very close to her. I actually kind of moved in. It was during my junior year of high school. I stayed with her for that whole year. I went away for the summer, which was a decision that a lot of people forced me to make. I needed not to get so involved with her death because I was young and vulnerable; she died that summer.

L) Sophie who?

T) Nacimiento. Her first husband was Brazilian. She always kept his name. He had wanted to go and fight fascism in Europe, but he was a known Communist. The Americans wouldn't let him enlist so he had to join the Merchant Marines. As a known Communist, my father wasn't able to fight. They isolated him in North Carolina, which was a terrible thing for him because he so wanted to be in the war. He was very committed to the ideas of fighting fascism and fighting Nazism. They never let him go to Germany until after the war. There were different kinds of things that happened to people who were open Communists. This was prior to the McCarthy era. What happened to Sophie's first husband was that she had contacted him and had heard from him—he was on a ship going back to the United States, then he disappeared. They had vaults on the ship that held the black book that captains always keep as the ship's diary. The diary disappeared. It was very suspicious; she was traumatized. She was traumatized until her sixties, when she died. She said it was the greatest trauma that she had ever experienced. Then she married Joe Lillard, and I knew them as a couple. He's a black American. She was very connected to all the issues that linked the need for social change to women and to blacks. She always said that women are leaders.

L) They weren't negative or downtrodden. They were strong. That's wonderful.

T) She was a great person. She left the party before many people left the party. She and her husband left it because she saw the problems within it—the hierarchy, the intellectualism, all the problems that later became much more exposed about the Communist Party. And she left it because of the ideological change that the Communist Party made on a national question about the black belt South, a very big issue for her, because the questions of empowerment and political power were fundamental to everything, and women and blacks had to have that. She died during the time of the Black Panther Party's creation. She thought that was great. She was very idealistic. It has hurt me a bit because she gave me such idealism. I wasn't prepared for the fact that the fight is so hard. When she was dying she believed that we were going to win. She told me that in a few years the fight would be over, and we'd win. But it's been so long. It's been sad. I understand why. She didn't do it to mislead me; she did it to inspire me to be idealistic.

L) To set your standards high. There is something to it. You always have to watch out. People are always there ready to buy you out, whenever you have a need. It's easy to sell.

T) I know. So it's nice that I have her great memory. She spoke about feminism as something that was like a shining light in our history as women, and as something that you bring to everything you do. Never to emulate men, always to do it in your own style. I was very fortunate, at such a young age, to have such an example. And she always encouraged me to be an artist; revolution without art is dangerous. She was right there all the time. I did sculpture then. As I told you, I got kicked out of school, while she was still alive, because I did three sculptures of women who were making love to each other. The high school freaked out, and they kicked me out. And even in that, she was able to say I was right. She was always filled with a very large vision, and to me, that's what feminism is. Feminism is not being defensive and it's not saying it's only for me. It's a very large vision of what is right for the largest percentage of people all over the world—which is women.

L) Too bad you didn't go to Nairobi. I've been speaking to people who did go. (I did not go.)

T) Did they have a great time?

L) It was complex. It was very political. Talk about idealism. Africa had its problems, and Nairobi had its police force, and they had their censorship. I heard from people that they had a constant film festival, showings of film and video; everything had to be submitted in advance to the Board of Censorship. I heard stories about films being cut up, literally, physically.

T) What was the thrust? What was the main thing they wanted to cut out?

L) I don't know if it was political or sexual. Your sculptures story is interesting because I would like to find out if they cut things about female sexuality out of the films; I don't know. And some things were just lost. They tried to pretend to be inept, apparently, but it wasn't ineptitude, it was politics.

T) Oh, sure.

L) But they did have a lot of films, anyway. I'm getting things, I've asked for a copy of the brochure.

T) Have you gone to Women Make Movies [a distributor] in New York City?

L) I've spoken to them, and I've met them. Debra Zimmerman is there, and I know people whose work they handle. Doris Chase, for example. But I haven't gone there yet.

T) I was on the board, and I'm in the transitional state of getting off the board. You must set your priorities—that's not the kind of work I want to do, being on a board. It necessitates investment of time. If you're going to do it, you've got to do it [completely]. That's not where I am; I'm trying really hard to find out where I am. Right now, the two key things are production and family, and it's hard, very hard. But after I had my last child, I kept my intense production schedule, and I was away a lot.

L) I've been thinking about this, too, the business of mother and artist. It's something I've been fascinated with. I think one of the reasons that the person as artist—the artist self, that part of us that creates art—goes into production is because we know that we have to be more than a mother. It's not a negative thing. I think that we use our artist self to assert dialectically against the mother role, because mother is often a role defined for us by others. My son used to tell me, "You have to do that because you're my mother." It's imposed. The mother role is so societal and is so much what your children want from you, what your family expects you to be in relation to your children, that it intensifies the contrapuntal need to be the artist. I don't think it's selfish; I think it's normal.

T) I don't think it's selfish but I think that there are times when you have to figure it out; maybe selfish is the wrong word, but there's got to be a way to have a healthy balance, which I don't think is easy to find. That has been really a huge struggle for me. Most of my friends who have made it in media are men. I'm serious. My husband always says that the biggest weakness in my life is that I haven't married a wife; that's the biggest glaring hole.

L) But you do have a communal living situation.

T) Yes, but, ultimately, I don't have a homemaker in the truest sense, and that's what every artist really needs.

My new piece on teenage unemployment is called *The Forgotten Ones*. You know why I named it *The Forgotten Ones*? You know Buñuel?

L) The Spanish director—*Los Olvidados*.

T) I love *Los Olvidados*, so I figured—what the hell—let's name it the same thing, but it has an analysis in it, not just the experience.

L) Do you stay connected with the people that you've worked with?

T) Oh, yes, very much. My work is often about the people I know; my husband is in the documentary about the post office. Now, my husband, Sean, works for the Transit Authority. He works for the New York subway system, and I have a new idea— to produce something about the urban "coal mine" which is the New York Transit Authority.

L) When we spoke on the phone the first time, you told me that you were interested in the issue of pay equity. It's something that I'm also very interested in. Believe me, it's a bread-and-butter issue for most women. I'm a librarian. In order even to walk through the door to get a job, I have to have a master's degree. Librarians get out of graduate school and walk into a job where they're often glad to earn $15,000 a year. In New Jersey now we have a minimum salary for teachers, kids with B.A.s who can walk out of any college and walk into a job for

$18,500. We're so demoralized, the library profession is blotto. This is a bread-and-butter issue.

T) It is, I think, a very important issue, because pay equity goes beyond the simple issue of what men and women earn. It's an across-the-board thing.

L) If it's done right, it can turn society upside down.

T) Let me ask you a question. If you were thinking in terms of a production, a documentary, how would you present it visually? You might be able to tell Lyn Goldfarb because you see it differently than Lyn does.

L) Maybe you'd have to go into a country where it's working. Maybe not in the United States.

T) Well, that's the problem. When I was sitting down with Lyn, and we were thinking hard about it—pay equity was not yet a visual thing—I felt that what's sellable about some of the things I've done in the past is the visual and the emotional, together with an idea and an intellectual message.

L) Tell me about your choice of the documentary form.

T) Over fiction?

L) Over so-called art or fiction.

T) The director of the Black Maria Film Festival and I have a running discussion. He separates documentary and art. I think there is art video as images; it's electronic, and it's art video. Yes, but documentary is also art.

L) Good. Let's hear about that.

T) I think that even a tape that trains people and has the very specific objective of training can be done creatively, artistically, and aesthetically. Art can be incorporated into everything. I don't make the distinction between documentary and art films and art video. I feel there's a real interrelationship between the media. The development of high-tech video art has a purpose and is valuable. People like Doris Chase are good examples of that. Unfortunately, we have oodles of examples of the emptiness of video art. I feel comfortable being able to say it because it's going to take a lot of daring to be able to use this high-tech stuff and keep it effectively artistic and not just thinking that glitzy colors and images and electronic impulses are going to be able to say something artistically.

L) What about women you know who have gotten caught in the quicksand? I can think of some women who when they were independent documentarists or independent art filmmakers were doing wonderful, exciting things that were never commercial successes. Then they went to Hollywood—Hollywood as a state of mind, not necessarily a place, commercial, high-tech and big budget—and lost some of the connectedness. Martha Coolidge. Did you see her new film *Real Genius*?

T) What's it about?

L) It's about a boy who gets a scholarship to go to college because he's a real genius; it's about his life. It's another teenage boy movie, and she was making feminist documentaries before. What happened to her? Who else did that? Claudia Weill was making feminist documentaries, and her first feature *Girlfriends* was an independently produced, low budget film. I hate to associate low budget and technological squeeze with good art, but . . .

T) What does she do now?

L) I don't know. She made a film called *It's My Turn* a couple of years ago, in the early 1980s. It was a studio backed film with stars, all of the fancy things and a higher budget, and she lost, to me, some of the connectedness.

T) It's hard.

L) Does it have to happen?

T) I don't think it has to happen. I definitely want to go in the direction of feature films. I like the idea of having more control and not having to work so much with spontaneity; that's what documentary is. The other thing is, I like drama, to be able to address human minds and human conditions. I want to put my own point across, not always other people's points of views, and that's what documentary is. In documentary, you have to let other people do their own talking. I really love it and believe in it, but I also want to do my own talking. I think if I had a script and if I were working with actors on a fictional piece, I'd have that much more control, though not that much more creativity. Documentary is as creative as fiction, in some cases more creative. I don't think it's a question that one is more creative than the other. Fiction definitely reaches a wider range of people because we're more conditioned to be receptive to fictional pieces, narrative pieces. I also feel that then there would be a real change because I would be totally in the driver's seat, or with the screenwriter or whomever, whatever the collaboration is.

L) Here's something that's been disturbing to me. I see a lot of films and a lot of television. The things that move me the most are usually documentaries that are beautifully made. What happens? Is the commercial scene so imbued with its own codes, traditions, and imperatives that when you enter into the language of commercial films, that whole world of commercial film, it starts stamping itself on you? Can you retain your individuality?

T) I think John Sayles does.

L) That's a good point.

T) I think he does. I don't think he's very daring politically, but *Brother from Another Planet* was very interesting. Lee Grant has been very true. I am thinking of a documentary she did, *Wilmar 8,* and then the wonderful fiction piece . . .

L) *Tell Me a Riddle?*

T) I think it's fantastic! Isn't that great?

L) I loved it.

T) The author criticized it. She thought it was too Hollywoodian. Isn't that what the criticism was?

L) Tillie Olsen said that she thought the story was changed in its focus from the internal psychological dialogue of the woman and her memory. It became much more Melvyn Douglas's film. And she felt that the actress, who was a wonderful actress in a lot of ways . . .

T) Oh, I think she's wonderful.

L) . . . was worried too much about her appearance and being beautiful and not enough about the internal aspect.

T) The older woman?

L) Yes, and that Melvyn Douglas became too important in the film. The point of Olsen's piece, which I read and reread after seeing the film, was different, but as a film it worked.

T) I actually like it better as a film than when I read it as a book. Film works so much better for me than books, but I thought it was pretty true, not exactly true to the short story, but to life. And I really liked it. I haven't seen Lee Grant. What is she doing now?

L) I don't know. I can't connect with her. She's a person I'm interested in interviewing, but I haven't been able to meet her.

T) She lives in New York. You should send her a letter about what you're doing.

L) Oh, I did.

T) You did?

L) Last year, maybe even longer ago, she was one of the first people I wanted to get to, but I haven't been able to get to her. Then I went to a place where she was due to speak—at Barnard—but she didn't show. Have you ever shown any work at the Barnard Film Festival, by the way?

T) No, I know about it. I should really take more initiative in doing that. I've never done it. I have never filled out the applications. That's a whole job unto itself, keeping up with that kind of dissemination to the festivals. I do think that Grant is working on something now, and I cannot remember what it is. But she's a good example of somebody who's good. And who else is pretty good? I don't know.

L) People who have crossed over from independent documentary.

T) Not many, because so few can cross over successfully. It's a very hard thing. The other thing is remaining an independent for too long. It's very hard for a lot of people I know who have been independent, who have been attracted to it and have gotten jobs at TV stations. I was recently in Minneapolis visiting a friend, a woman, a feminist, who produced wonderful films. She produced the videotape *Take Back the Night* and the first Take Back the Night demonstrations in Minneapolis.

L) What's her name?

T) Kathy Seltzer. She's produced a few other things. I'll give you information on how to reach her. But the problem is (and I say "the problem" though it's a contradiction because I also say women have to know technology, but I believe that women and blacks and Hispanics have to be more educated than white men; we have to know everything because we will be tested and challenged), right now Kathy is at a local PBS station in Minneapolis, learning CMX, a very high technology computer editing, and ADO editing. I hope she doesn't get stuck there because the phenomenon is, once you start making $30,000, $40,000, $45,000 . . .

L) And you have benefits and you have security.

T) . . . it's very hard to go back to being an independent.

L) You get used to all those comforts, and you need them, too. It's risky.

T) I have many friends who have left the independent community. They might be working for Channel 4, they might be working for ABC . . .

L) But can they transform ABC or Channel 4 once they're there? Can they retain their feminism and their independent points of view and make good shows?

T) One or two shows can be very good, but they can't do it all the time because of the system. All the stations are stations of the system.

L) You can't work from within the system?

T) Well, I think you can.

L) Is PBS different?

T) No, I don't think PBS is different. PBS is just a big rat race like the rest.

L) What about WGBH in Boston?

T) A few more women producers, a few more social documentaries come out of there, very select. They basically do not promote, do not work with, they negate the existence of the American independent community, and that's PBS, nationwide.

L) What about the program series "Independent Focus"?

T) Independent Focus is a token, a token gesture. Stroke the American filmmakers, push us all into one program, don't integrate us into the main body, use BBC.

L) Sort of an independent ghetto.

T) Exactly. Now, it grew out of a good thing. It grew out of the independent community's lobbying. PBS did not knock on our door and say, "Do you want this?" It grew out of people fighting with PBS and then getting it. The Association of Independent Video and Filmmakers is the lifeblood of the independent community, an important organization for us, and it was out of the very early years of AIVF that Independent Focus evolved, through a lot of effort.

L) They got that and what happened? AIVF stopped pushing?

T) No, no, AIVF keeps pushing; it's just very hard. Global Village was doing an interview, and they called me because they wanted some information for an article about the future of independents. I said that I think that fewer and fewer people will become independent producers as the money gets scarcer. But independent production usually lends itself to socially oriented media, video and film productions. And more of that is needed now. It's a really sad situation. Yet we have less resources. It's very frustrating out there. A lot of people feel the need for security, which is something that becomes greater as we grow older.

L) If you have a family that's true. How about health insurance?

T) You can buy it from AIVF now. They're trying to give everything; it's a very valuable association. But I think fewer and fewer people can remain in the independent community solely doing independent productions. So a lot of women and a lot of minorities have gotten other jobs. And getting other jobs, the attraction is twofold. It's partly the stability and the income, and it's partly the glitz, the neon furniture that we watch, to be inside the booths, inside the editing room, the control rooms and the studios that create this.

L) It's really fun, though; that is fun to do. You must know that. You must know that playing with the medium itself is fun.

T) It has to be totally integrated into the real world; it has to be part of everything in the real world. Cuba used to make its violinists cut sugar cane. When I was in Cuba, a lot of people fought against it because they said a violinist can't play the violin well with calloused hands. But they can get to know those who listen to music and the pain of the sugar cane worker; they can reflect that in their music only if they cut cane. I'm a believer in that. I've never separated art from the people, because then you end up having what we have in this country, alienated art, alienated artists, people who leave art, become video technicians. It's a sad phenomenon. I always say if I can't support myself doing this, I'll become a waitress or a cook. Becoming a technician or technocrat in some **PBS** editing room would be such a defeat.

L) There's your idealism coming from Sophie again. But it has shaped your vision of yourself, your identity, who you want to be, and it comes through in your work. Before I met you, I was rehearsing in my mind the kinds of things I wanted to talk about; I didn't have to because you were ready to talk. I never know. But I was sure that I needed to talk to you, just having seen your work, and I talked to Christine Vogel a little bit about you because the work is socially connected. It's juicy, it's right there, you don't have to worry about it. Whatever skills you might get working in technology shouldn't worry you. You're so grounded in people, it's so clear, that even if you had another couple of layers of technical glitz, it wouldn't kill that because it's really there in your work. Whereas someone else might just fly off.

T) I would like to play with feature film. So would Lyn Goldfarb. We both talk about that.

L) What would you do? Would you write your own story?

T) Oh, maybe I would work with a writer and collaborate on ideas. I think I'd rather collaborate. I've always wanted to do it about the commonplace woman. Not the unusual, but the woman who takes the Path train every day, who picks up the baby at the day care center—to look at women like that and their lives.

L) Something around here though? Did you read *The Beans of Egypt Maine?* It's about grinding rural poverty. It's filled with horrible and abrasive images and also a lot of beauty because the landscape is so beautiful. Even while they're suffering people can see the beauty.

T) That's interesting.

L) Brutal.

T) But in Maine?

L) It's by a woman named Carolyn Chute. It's her first novel. Maybe sometimes when you're thinking of making a movie, you can find a text.

T) Exactly. Somebody just got a text they want to work with, and they got in touch with the writer, and I think it's free. I've always wanted to do *Freedom Road* by Howard Fast.

L) I know his work, but not that book.

T) I loved that piece. Mostly male characters in it, and then there were a few pieces, *Daughters of Earth*? Is that the name, by Smedley? Or *Daughter of the Earth*?

L) Agnes.

T) Agnes Smedley. She's an American who was very connected to Indian independent movement, but *Daughter of Earth*, that's the name of it. It's about Appalachia and it's autobiographical. It's about her growing up there and the conditions there. I definitely have thought that that would be a good way to start. To connect with a novel, work with someone, and work with a woman writer to try and develop something. It would be very hard to get something like that funded, but I would like to do it.

L) Does the Guggenheim Foundation support fiction?

T) Anything. I could go in any direction, but I've already mapped out the use of this money . . .

L) Is there more there? Will you go back to them and say, "Hey, this was nice, now I need more"?

T) I don't know if you can. I didn't ask that.

L) How do you get things funded if you don't want to go to the studio system? How does Woody Allen get funding?

T) I don't know. God, he's so wealthy.

L) Yes, but how did he do it before he was wealthy? How did he get started? How do they do it in Europe?

T) But that's just it, definitely a jump to the feature, to fiction. A lot of my friends feel the same way. Lorraine Gray's also working on a big documentary about women. You might want to interview her.

L) Where is she?

T) Lyn could help you. I don't really know her—I met her a few times. She's working on a documentary about women in the international economy called *The Global Assembly Line*, and she's been all over the world shooting. Another person you should definitely interview is Kieko Tsuno of DCTV. She's a Japanese producer and director. Her work is wonderful. I would also like to suggest Kathy Seltzer. She has done a couple of pieces. She's a feminist, and her work really reflects that. She's away from it now but it might still be valuable. I'll leave it to you to make that decision. You can mention my name, saying that you spoke with me. I have just seen her. I'm trying to think of who else. Lyn Goldfarb, who's going to be calling me soon. She's a wonderful, wonderful person.

L) I thought so from her work.

T) And she's very committed to the issues. Do you know Julia Gustafson from Global Village, the video center in the city? Julia is one of the directors. Her husband's name is John. She's produced a thing about natural childbirth. I'm trying to think of more women who make movies, how many active producers are there? Have you spoken to DeeDee Halleck?

L) She taught at Rutgers.

T) Well, DeeDee Halleck recently—at AIVF's 10th Anniversary—got an award as advocate for the independent producer. DeeDee is an innovator, she's fought for public access, she has a public access show that was recently at the Whitney Museum, called *Paper Tiger Television*. She produced a show called *Waiting for the Invasion* that's about Nicaragua. She's very colorful, and very important. You should very definitely speak to her. Do you know Barbara Koppel?

L) I know *Harlan County*, I don't know her. Do you see her?

T) Well, she's in New York City. Oh, Debbie Schaefer, do you know Debbie Schaefer?

L) I think I do.

T) Debra Schaefer is a key person, a very important, full-time independent producer, an excellent producer, socially committed, who does film and video. She doesn't have kids, she doesn't have obstacles. Okay, Debbie Schaefer works with Skylight Productions sometimes.

L) Barbara Koppel works with which production company?

T) Cabincreek Productions. Debra Schaefer did the recent thing with Dr. Clemente about El Salvador; he was a doctor who was in Vietnam and then he was in El Salvador and become politicized. Before that she did *The Wobblies.*

L) I know *The Wobblies.*

T) She also did the documentary *El Salvador, Another Vietnam.* Very important. Another very important woman.

L) Where is she?

T) New York City. She's a filmmaker, fundamentally. She does video secondarily. Another important person is Pam Yates. She did *When Mountains Tremble* about Guatemala. *From the Ashes* was done by Helena Soberg-Ladd. Have you met her?

L) Everytime I call her, she's filming out of town. She's important, too.

T) She's very good. She's a nice person.

L) Is Pam Yates in New York now?

T) I think she's in and out of New York. These people work very differently than I do.

L) They're always going all over the world.

CHRONOLOGY

AMALIE R. ROTHSCHILD

Amalie Rothschild, 1980.

154 Amalie R. Rothschild

Amalie R. Rothschild was born in Baltimore, Maryland, on June 3, 1945, to Randolph Schamberg and Amalie Getta (Rosenfeld) Rothschild. She has a B.F.A. from Rhode Island School of Design (1967) and a M.F.A. in motion picture production from New York University (1969).

She has produced and directed nine films including *Woo Who? May Wilson* (1969); *It Happens to Us* (1971); *Nana, Mom and Me* (1974); and *Conversations with Willard Van Dyke* (1981).

Rothschild did special effects cinematography for three years for the Joshua Light Show at the Fillmore East Theater in New York City and was on the staff at the 1969 Woodstock Festival. She worked extensively as a free-lance photographer in the music field; her photographs were published by *Time-Life Books, The New York Times, Newsweek, The Village Voice, Rolling Stone,* Warner Bros. records, and many other publications. A 30-page section of her photographs was included in the 1972 Bobbs-Merrill book *The Photography of Rock.*

While working on a film about legalized abortion, she began to recognize the importance of distribution for independent filmmakers and with Julia Reichert, Jim Klein and Liane Brandon helped organize and found New Day Films, the first successful nontheatrical distribution cooperative.

Rothschild has been a consultant and panelist for the Youthgrant Program of the National Endowment for the Humanities, a founder and Board Member of both The Association of Independent Video and Filmmakers and Independent Cinema Artists and Producers, and a Trustee of International Film Seminars, for whom she helped initiate

and organize the highly successful 1976 Conference on 16-mm Distribution, co-sponsored by The
Educational Film Library Association.

She has taught production at New York University's Undergraduate Institute of Film and Television.
She is listed in *Who's Who of American Women,
Who's Who in the East,* and the *World Who's Who
of Women.*

She coordinated and edited *Doing It Yourself: A
Handbook on Independent Distribution.* She has received production grants from The New York State
Council on the Arts (2), The National Endowment
for the Arts (5), The Maryland Arts Council, The
Ohio Joint Program in the Arts and Humanities,
The American Film Institute, and many private
foundations. She is a frequent lecturer at colleges,
universities, and civic and other groups.

Her film, *Conversations with Willard Van Dyke,*
won the Best award in Fine Arts and the Bronze
award at the 1981 San Francisco International Film
Festival, was acquired by the British Broadcasting
Corporation, and is being distributed by both the
British Film Institute and the Australian Film Institute. This film initiated more than eight months of
international travel at the invitation of film festivals
in Australia, New Zealand, Scotland, England, Italy,
and India. In addition, Rothschild has presented
screening/lecture programs for the United States
Information Service in Turkey, New Zealand, In-
donesia, Hong Kong, and the People's Republic of
China.

She has had a one-woman show at the Film
Forum in New York, a Museum of Modern Art
Cineprobe show, and a three-day retrospective at
the Sheldon Film Theatre and Art Gallery in Lin-

coln, Nebraska. Margaret Mead invited her to include her film *Nana, Mom and Me* to the 1977 Kin and Communities symposium at the Smithsonian Institution.

Her work has been part of the New American Filmmakers Series at the Whitney Museum, is included in the American Federation of the Arts catalogue, and is available through New Day Films and the Cinema Guild. Her films are in widespread distribution in the United States and Canada, and have been shown on public and cable television and in many national and international film festivals including those in London, Edinburgh, Sydney, Rotterdam, Fesival dei Popli, FILMEX, and New York. Excerpts of *Woo Who? May Wilson* and *It Happens to Us* have been shown on NBC and ABC network television.

She is fluent in Italian and divides her time between residences in New York City and Rome, Italy.

Besides new film projects, Rothschild also continues to work as a still photographer and graphic designer.

INTERVIEW

Interview on April 6, 1983, with Amalie Rothschild, director of *It Happens to Us; Nana, Mom and Me; Woo Who? May Wilson;* and other films.

L) I'm interested in the fact that you own everything that you need in order to do a complete job from beginning to end. Do you want to tell me about having all the facilities? And how you got them?

A) Can you imagine a writer not owning a typewriter?

L) Yes, I guess I can.

A) No, if you're going to be able to do your work, you need to own as much of your own equipment as possible, because it gives you the freedom to have your tools available to you all the time. I don't use them all the time; in fact, one of my main sources of support and income is renting my facilities to other people when I'm not in production. Because of the nature and difficulty of raising money to do independent work in the first place, I am actually *not* in production more than I'm *in* production. My image of the lifestyle, or the life, of the independent filmmaker—my own in particular—is the Myth of Sisyphus; every film is another fresh rock at the bottom of an increasingly steep hill. The hill always seems to get steeper. What one would hope, desire, wish, dream is that after you've done a couple of films and gotten a little bit of recognition for the work, that at least people would accept the fact that you know how to make films.

157

L) Do you feel as if you're still proving that?

A) You have to prove it every single time, all over again, as if it's practically your first work—not quite. . . .

L) Is that because you're an independent? Or because you're a woman, because you're a documentarist, or a little of all of the above?

A) I think it's all of the above and other factors that perhaps aren't connected to any of them, but simply the whole nature of the financing of noncommercial work in this country.

L) These are the things that interest me. One is that you *can* do it. One of the women I talked to, Doris Chase, is a video artist and has been a filmmaker, and it's interesting to see the kinds of compromises that she has to make because she doesn't own her own studio facilities for video postproduction. She has to get into somebody else's studio.

A) Having not only that inconvenience, which is terrible, it also means that from day one, every time you have something that you want to do, you have added in all kinds of additional organizational work in order to get hold of the equipment that you want, in order to negotiate the length of time that it's available to you. You organize and plan your life either around the stuff that you rent and set up in your own premises for the duration of that particular project or else, the more common thing is that, people, when they're starting out (and I've made my services available at very little cost or, on rare occasions, at no cost to people who are doing "worthy" work or whom I know), have to arrange to use other people's equipment in the middle of the night and around their own schedule, which is a real hassle and requires so much more energy from you. You're asking questions that I haven't thought much about before, but what comes to mind is something that I've acknowledged only to myself, which is why I can put it into words, but it's curious. The fact that I have all my own equipment and have spent a lot of energy in creating a facility within which I can work is a concept, an idea, desire, need, or whatever that's part of the legacy I get from my mother. I grew up in a house where it was taken for granted that you had the tools available to you in your own environment to do what you did. It was always an assumption that one way or another I would eventually acquire what I needed to work with, to have my own set-up. I think that there's financial wisdom in that as well. That I have owned basically everything that I need for 16-millimeter production has enabled me to make films that I might otherwise not have been able to make. I can always cut corners and budgets, and actually produce a work with substantially less cash than I otherwise would. People with conventional financial wisdom say that that's not true because you have to amortize the cost of equipment, and you had to lay out the capital to buy it in the first place, and so on. Yes, that's true, except that doesn't account for how in fact I was able to do this, because with the exception of my Steenbeck and my Steenbeck rewind table, which I bought new, every other piece of equipment that I own (that means five synchronizers, sets of rewinds, projector editing benches, trim bins, split reels, splicers, my Nagra, tripods, every other piece of hard gear) I bought at auction at a fraction of its value, because I've always been a bargain hunter and a shopper.

L) Did you learn that from your mother, too?

A) No, that I picked up on my own. And I was also fortunate enough to get the Steenbeck in 1971 before the price trebled. I paid $10,000 for my Steenbeck. The current price for the comparable machine is $28,000 and climbing.

L) Still a lot of money—$10,000.

A) Yes, but I had it—I earned that money. I got my Steenbeck with money from a business deal with John Lennon and Yoko Ono from my rock-and-roll days.

L) That's another thing. I know you've told this story often, too, but could you just remind me about how you made the transition from photographer to filmmaker? You were working as a photographer?

A) It wasn't a direct transition. I fell in love with movies when I was twelve years old. During my undergraduate days at Rhode Island School of Design, I became the president of the film society and went to movies all the time. I saw on average a film a day during all my undergraduate years, but it never occurred to me to be a filmmaker.

L) Why?

A) Lots of reasons. First of all, I was majoring in graphic design and still photography and it was in fact my work in photography that was primary. I actually began taking pictures seriously in high school when I was the art editor of our yearbook and found that the staff photographers simply weren't taking the pictures that I wanted; they didn't respond to my direction. In desperation, I took a camera and started taking the pictures my- self, but was absolutely, overwhelmingly intimi- dated by the mystique of the technology involved in processing and printing.

L) But the will preceded the skill? That's in- teresting.

A) I also had that background in my family. As you recall, my mother's a visual artist. My father is a very good amateur photographer, as you can see in *Nana, Mom and Me.* All of the 8-millimeter home movies shown in the film were taken by my father, even the one where he's in the shots. He would set up the camera, get everything in line, and then get in the picture.

L) You were watching him doing that all those years?

A) Well, no, he stopped doing that when I was five years old, so I can't attribute it to that, but it's osmosis. It's in the atmosphere.

L) My grandfather was a professional pho- tographer. I'm not, but I've retained the interest in all the visual arts. I used to watch him developing. But I know what you mean.

A) At R.I.S.D. I had my first formal course in photography, which included the darkroom, and that got me through the mystique of the technol- ogy. I found it was simple, startlingly simple for me at least, and I began to think that maybe this wasn't so difficult after all. If someone as dumb as I thought I was could figure it out, then it couldn't be as hard as I had imagined it was.

L) Had you been drawing and painting all along?

A) Always, always. I was going to be an artist like my mother.

L) If that was easy, I should imagine technology would be, too. To me, drawing is the hardest thing to do.

A) I went to R.I.S.D. thinking that I would go into painting and be an artist, a fine artist, a visual artist like my mother, but I soon discovered that I felt that I could not draw well enough, nor was I centered enough visually to feel that I had anything to say or images to make that obsessed me enough. I ended up with graphic design as a major, which is advertising design, layout and posters, commercial art of a certain kind. Photography was a compulsory course, it was a part of it. Once I took that course, I concentrated more on photography than on graphics. I was a good student. I got As and Bs, did very well, but not without enormous battles because there was a very, very competitive atmosphere at the school. I was made to feel extremely inferior. No matter what I did, it wasn't good enough; it was a real struggle. I learned years later that those perceptions were valid because there was enormous prejudice there against women. I'm one of the few women in my class who has straightforwardly pursued a professional career.

L) Were there any women on the faculty?

A) Not in my major. There were women on

the faculty. Most of the ones that I remember taught nature drawing.

L) Flowers, trees?

A) Trees and birds and animals and still life, that sort of thing. Yes, there are women on the faculty now.

L) Now.

A) And a memorable experience during my freshman year at R.I.S.D. was a required course, Orthographic Projection Drawing, which is a drafting skill, and highly technical. It so happens I was very good in math. In fact, I was far superior in math than English in my college boards, and was always spatially, technically oriented. There was this very Prussian male teacher. My recollection of him is he would have looked very good as a Nazi in a movie.

L) Casting.

A) Yes, he was right out of central casting. I got an A− from him. He would hang around, he would watch me in class; when I turned in my projects he would always scratch his head and say, "You're really doing this yourself, I can see that, but I don't believe it. I've never met another woman in all my experience that could do this." I was the first woman that he'd ever given an A of any kind to, ever, and he'd been teaching that course for about twelve years.

L) And he couldn't find an excuse not to give you an A.

A) He gave me an A—. At the time, it was a matter of pride for me. I had no feminist consciousness. This was in 1963. But I remembered it very vividly years later after the women's movement existed, and I began to see the context within which those things fit.

L) In those days, we just didn't know what they were really saying to us.

A) No, we didn't, and all those years I felt inferior. I felt no matter what I did, it was directly, personally, specifically I who just couldn't quite cut it. Now it is possible for me to see how much of that was just a matter of prejudice. Luckily for me my chief character trait, and the one that I was most put down for, that which they tried to destroy in me as I was growing up, but which I realize now is the one thing that enabled me to survive, is my determined stubbornness.

L) Assertiveness as they say.

A) Something in me was strong enough so that no matter what happened, some part of me never quite believed that I could really be so bad, that I should give up, should quit. I don't know if that has anything to do with heredity or anything else; I'm not saying this to try to give myself any credit for it. Perhaps it has something to do with a quirk of biology. The film *Nana, Mom and Me* was one way of my looking at my roots and trying to explore some of the forces in my background, how I got to be me. I've been doing that in general, not just in the course of making that film, and I've come to see that my family on both sides was comprised of incredibly strong women, many of whom were hated because they were so tough-minded. So I think biology does have something to do with it.

L) And example—biology and example. But I do think kids are born a certain way, from the moment that they're born.

A) Yes. I mean, you have to weigh in dispositions.

L) So you were not really a filmmaker yet, then. I mean, you're there. You're not even thinking particularly about filmmaking. But you're definitely a photographer.

A) I'm a photographer, and I'm a movie lover. I got into the European honors program during my senior year at R.I.S.D. That meant that I lived in Italy for a year, in Rome. As soon as I arrived, I immediately found out where all the private cinema clubs were and began going to the movies. These were private cinema clubs where people like Rossellini and Bellocchio would bring double system cuts of works in progress to the private audience. Although I was too shy to speak it, I was learning Italian well enough to get a lot out of it anyway.

L) Was this taking a risk at that age, just getting up and going to Rome for a year, or was it something that a lot of people do from your school?

A) Only twenty-five students out of two hundred were selected to go.

L) That's pretty unusual and special.

A) That was one of the reasons that I selected R.I.S.D. as my first choice of college. Not only did it have about the best art school reputation in the country at the time, but it also had the European honors program. There would be this possible opportunity to spend a year in Europe, which I very much wanted to do. I knew that from high school.

L) You knew you were a traveler, even if you didn't know you were a filmmaker.

A) I've always wanted to travel. It was during that year in Rome that everything gelled. All my friends knew what a film buff I was and how crazy I was about movies. They took it for granted that I was going to end up in film in some capacity. It came about when I was walking home one night with a girl friend. I forget the context of the whole conversation, but she said she expected to see my name on the screen one day. And I said to her, "You're crazy; what are you talking about?" It seemed to be impossible. It never entered my mind.

L) I'm still trying to figure out why it seemed so impossible.

A) Well, girls didn't do that. At that time, once I looked into it and thought about it, there were two women filmmakers whom I knew of. They were Agnes Varda and Shirley Clark. They were the only ones that anybody, at that time, had ever heard of. This was September 1966 to May 1967. Anyhow, when she said that, I discounted it. Then I began to think about it a lot, about why I had discounted it, and then I thought, why not? This really planted the seed, and let my ego out of the bag.

L) You weren't intimidated by the technology any more because you had mastered photography.

A) Yes. But I didn't know anything about film. At that time, the only movie camera I had ever heard of was a Bolex. That's how ignorant I was. At the same time that I saw movies frequently and knew lots about them intellectually, historically, I still didn't know anything about how they were made, what the equipment was. I was fascinated by it, of course.

L) But in Rome you were taking a lot of pictures.

A) Oh, I did a whole book on photography. I had a darkroom and that was my thesis, a photography project, several photography projects. But, anyhow, that was what planted the seed of, well, why hadn't I thought of working in films? Of course, this is what I wanted to do. But at that point, the extent of the idea was, well, I'm a graphic artist, and that's what I know, that's what I'm good at, but there's a place for this in the film industry and that would be perfect, to get into working in films with my graphics background. I then began to look around for role models. I discovered that there were several people whose work I'd been looking at for a long time that I really, really admired. That was exactly the kind of thing I felt equipped to do in film, cinemagraphics. Saul Bass, Maurice Binder, and Elinor Bunin were three people at that time who were doing all these great, spiffy, fancy title sequences for films. That was the point at which it occurred to me that I needed to get technical background and training, that maybe it would be a good idea after R.I.S.D. to go to film school for graduate work, to acquire the skills to enable me to get into the business some way, as a handmaiden with my graphic skills. That was how it all came about that I applied to the NYU Film School; their new School of the Arts program was just getting started.

L) Who was there then? I can't remember.

A) It was a good class. There were thirty-four people in the class, six of whom were women. Out of those six women, four of us have sustained really productive careers. Muffy Meyer, Suzanne Baumann, and myself, the three of us, and there's another woman who dropped out, but who has continued to work, so far as I know, reasonably successfully as an editor. She didn't graduate.

L) Was there anybody on the faculty who was particularly helpful?

A) No, that came later.

L) This was a separate school. There were always cinema studies, but was this filmmaking?

A) Film production is always separate from cinema studies.

L) Although I know that there is cross-registration.

A) Only occasionally for courses, but not officially. Whatever cross-reference or cross-fertilization there is resides solely in the curiosity of the few individual students who take advantage of it. At least when I was there it was not encouraged. It's unusual when it occurs. Perhaps it's changed today. When I applied to NYU and went for my interview, I didn't know whether I going to be accepted. I went home to Baltimore for the summer to earn some money. There's a little complicated personal story which is entwined with all this, of how I got my first job. I had to earn money to pay for my round-trip airfare to Romania, to go back there for a month in August of 1967. I knew I had to work that summer. When I got home to Baltimore, I put my portfolio together and went traipsing around the city. I ended up going for an interview at the only commercial TV house in the whole city. They hired me on the spot to do graphics and be a kind of gal friday. They paid $75.00 a week, and that seemed a fortune to me.

L) That's what they paid me for my first job in publishing, back in 1960.

A) Yes. This was 1967.

L) I was thrilled to make it, too.

A) At that time, it was *the* fantasy dream job that I was looking for, that job that I was lucky to get. If I conceived of anything at that time of what I wanted to do, and be, at work, that was it. It wasn't just being a gal friday. I was setting up. They were teaching me everything. It was an apprenticeship. I learned how to use an Arriflex and load magazines....

L) And they let you do everything? Touch all the machines?

A) That's right, and use the old movieola upright. I was watching, and I did everything, plus they put me to work creatively. I made all kinds of props and stuff for commercials. I ran film to the lab. I went with them when they shot animation. I came to New York for my first meeting with Lee Dichter at *Photo Mag.* I was introduced to everything. Although I didn't know it at the time, my instincts were completely right. I was good, I stayed overtime, and I did everything that they wanted to perfection. Because I was enthralled with it all, I succeeded and learned a great deal.

L) And you were still photographing?

A) I was doing photography in there, too. Then I found out that I was accepted at film school and had to choose. They wanted to hire me full-tme on staff, and have me set up and run the cinemagraphics department. They offered me $125.00 a week to start, and I spent about a month changing my mind every other day about whether to come to New York and go to film school, or stay in Baltimore and work at this commercial firm. My mother encouraged me to come to New York and go to school. I think it was more her influence that helped convince me.

L) Why did she help you make that decision, do you think? What was her rationale?

A) Well, this was commercials, and I think it was several-fold. First, all her life she wanted to live in New York, and she knew New York was the place to be, and that I wasn't giving myself a chance by staying in a job of that kind. No matter how much I learned, inevitably, I would be very limited, and that by going to school, I had an opportunity to explore. I think it was very good judgment, and I'm grateful to her for that.

L) How come you listened to her? That's an interesting question.

A) I've always listened to my mother. In spite of our difficulties, and we have had them, she's got her head in the right place. She's been my strongest supporter, critic, and competitor. If you come to weighing and sifting it all out, now that I've come through it all and feel strong and good, for the things that have really counted, she's always given me the best advice.

L) Did you ever play with the notion of what it would have been like if you'd done it the other way? Because so many people do. The woman I was talking to this morning tried film school, didn't like it, and decided to work since she had the opportunity to work as an editor and slowly move up to being a producer and director. Did you ever speculate? Do you think you could have ended up in the same place?

A) I might have. I don't know. I will never know. I do know, however, that there have been several times in my life when I've come to a real crossroads. I've been fortunate in this sense because I had opportunities, and I've had choices to make. Many people don't have the opportunities at all. When I've come to a crossroads where I really had a very profound choice to make, I've made the right choices for the time.

L) You have no regrets?

A) It's more than not having regrets. I know I've made the right choice, I know that I've taken the right fork in the road that's led me to the next fork and slowly allowed me to build my life in the direction that I have always hoped it would take. It's been very rocky and very difficult at times, but I find I can survive, and each thing has pushed me, even when I'm not aware of it, in the right direction.

So I know going to school was right, and I don't know whether I would have been able to grow into the kind of person that I have been always groping towards becoming, if I had stayed in that job. My gut feeling is that I wouldn't have.

L) You were in school and you were learning production. Did you get your hands on much hard-line experience as you would have if you'd stayed working? Maybe you did.

A) A lot of people come to me for advice, and this is always a surprise to me when they do. One of the major things that I'm often asked is whether I think film school is worthwhile.

L) I guess it's the same question.

A) My answer is that I think there are many, many ways for people to get the kind of experience and knowledge necessary to be filmmakers. Film school is definitely not the only way, and I think it's questionable in many, many cases, probably the majority of cases. It certainly is meaningless so far as the business goes. But it's not like becoming a doctor where if you don't go to medical school, forget it, the profession doesn't exist for you. Film is still one of those professions where having a degree is meaningless. It has nothing to do with who's going to hire you or why. In relation to film school generally I advise women to take advantage of it. I think that it offers a unique environment for women to get hands-on experience and prove what they can do. Unless they come from extremely wealthy families or have some other extraordinary set of circumstances aiding them, women simply don't have the opportunities available to them in the working world that a clever, persevering, strong-minded, directed, goal-oriented man has.

L) Is the other side of that perhaps that women need more credentials in order to do the same thing?

A) I wouldn't define it directly as credentials—although I think that's accurate—because it isn't that film school gives you credentials, it doesn't. However, and this is the whole point, it's the classic "Catch-22." How can you make films if you've never made a film? If you know what you want to do and take advantage of the film school situation, you can make a film there, and that's what you need.

L) Did you do that?

A) Yes, I made *Woo Who? May Wilson.* It was my thesis film. It was the first film I ever made, and I made it in film school. Under no other circumstances in the world would I ever, by the broadest stretch of the imagination, have been able to make that film otherwise.

L) I love that film, I love that woman. I really want to find out what happened to her and why you picked her and how you found her. Did you meet her when you were living in the city and going to school?

A) No, she's from Baltimore. She and my mother used to exhibit in the same cooperative art gallery. I knew her when I was in high school, and I was fascinated by her.

L) Is she still alive?

A) Yes, she's still alive. She has severe diabetes and has become pretty reclusive, but she's still living in the same place and doing the same kind of work and is pretty well. (Note: May Wilson died on October 22, 1986, at the age of eighty-one.)

L) She wasn't that old. Not as old as Alice Neel.

A) I had been interested in her for some time.

L) You were able to distribute and market that film, everything, while you were in school?

A) No, no. I graduated in 1969; I finished the film the same year. When I moved to New York in 1967 and started at NYU Film School, I knew that May was living here, and I looked her up. We became friends. In the academic year at NYU we had seven weeks of classroom study and then ten weeks of production per semester. During the seven weeks of classroom study you had to scriptwrite, of course; everybody had to put together scripts. Then there was a faculty panel that included one or two student representatives who went through all the scripts and selected those which would be produced during the ten-week production period.

L) And that means that they invested in the equipment?

A) The school owned the equipment.

L) But those were the people who would have access to it.

A) The people whose scripts were selected were the directors of their projects, and those were the films that were going to be made that semester. So the first semester of my second year, starting September 1968, was documentary scriptwriting, and I chose May as the subject for my script. I taped interviews with her and transcribed them and organized them essentially into the film that I actually made. I used her voice. I ran the voice-over down one side of the page and on the other side of the page described what we would see; it was selected as one of the films to be produced that semester. That's how I got my chance to make my movie. It was budgeted by the school to be a ten-minute film, and they allocated about $600 toward its production; then I made it. I never intended to make it a short film; it was always going to be about a half-hour. I just went ahead and made a thirty-three-minute film. I finished it after I had already graduated. We graduated in June 1969, and I had my first answer print in September 1969. I ended by having to put about $2,000 of my own money into it. The film combines my background in the visual arts with my new-found filmmaking. It's about a visual artist. I used her work, which I animated in the film. I used my graphic background as well as my still photography background, because I took all of the stills that I animated in the film as well, and designed and photographed the title sequence.

L) I love your titles. You really have an eye for that. So when did you work at the Fillmore and work with the rock-and-roll people?

A) Well, the Fillmore East Theatre shared a wall with NYU Film School, and I was also working on other people's films.

L) Other students' films?

A) Other students' films, yes. A film made before my own was one that Muffy Meyer made about two thirteen-year-old would-be groupies who were really just innocent rock-and-roll star worshipers. I can give a very clear chronology of how all the events in my life connected, led me from one place to the next. Going back to the technical aspect of film, once I got over thinking that I was incapable of understanding the technology, which occurred in the first photography course, I immediately, like a duck takes to water, became fascinated and wanted to know everything. At film school I then began to hang out with all the guys in the equipment room. However, I encountered a lot of difficulty. First of all, I had been raised with the attitude, "don't touch it, you'll break it." That was one of the reasons it was so hard to overcome the mental attitude that technology was beyond me.

L) Even with your mother's being an artist?

A) My mom is good with her hands, with using mechanical tools like a table saw, an electric drill. But that's a far cry from the new electronic technology and computers. So that was the message that came through loud and clear. We all know there are differences between verbal and nonverbal communication. At film school I hung around the technicians, which was difficult only because I had to be really persistent to get them to take me seriously.

L) These were the people who did the project and . . .

A) . . . repaired the equipment and so forth.

L) I supervise a whole crew of them at work.

A) In school I had been working on everybody else's films, doing props and posters, doing backgrounds, taking photographs, and I started using cameras, that was my big interest—shooting, cinematography. The camera repair and maintenance technician for the film school was also an audio engineer who worked at the Fillmore. One day he was going over there, and I said, "Can I come along?" He said, "Sure." I went along and walked in there for the first time. This was within a couple of weeks after it opened. When I walked into that theater and up in the sound booth, I saw a poster on the wall that I had designed and made for one of our student productions. I just immediately had a feeling that I belonged in that place and that I'd been there before. So I began to hang out there. At first I just got some free passes for some of the shows, and I'd come with my still camera and started photographing. My most vivid early memory was the first concert that Joni Mitchell played there. I had never heard her before. I thought she was wonderful.

L) And she still is.

A) Oh, yes. Then, at Fillmore, I began to become really mesmerized by the light show. I'd never seen anything like it. I thought it was fantastic, what they were doing visually as an accompaniment to the music. It was exciting and wonderful. By then I was pals with the guys who worked there. They gave me passes and I came there often. I was like a technical groupie, as it were. I wasn't a groupie;

I never slept with anybody. It was the technical aspect of it, though, that was fascinating to me. That lasted for a couple of months until I had a run-in with the chief security guy at the theater. He decided that I didn't belong there and threw me out, and said, "You'll never get in here again." I said to myself, "That's what you think." And that's when I decided I was going to work there. I put together a portfolio and went to see Josh of the Joshua Light Show and convinced him to hire me for the light show, to do films and graphics because that's where I saw they were weak and could use somebody to do that for them. He hired me. That happened within twenty-four hours. I came back the next night with my staff pass and stuck my tongue out at the security guy.

L) The uses of anger. It really helps.

A) It's happened a lot in my life. Somebody's really tried to block me with a "You can't do that," and I say, "That's what you think." I'll never take "no" for an answer.

L) I love it. I love it.

A) And then I started to work there.

L) And you said you took pictures of everybody.

A) Except the Beatles. I became the unofficial staff house photographer, covering everything backstage, and onstage, and in the audience.

L) You said you had considered doing a book. Have you considered doing a book about that period?

A) Yes, that's what I'm starting to work on now, because it's time for it, and I've got about 20,000 color negatives.

L) Now that the 1960s and 1970s are officially history.

A) Well, I think that now the time is right for a really good coffee table quality book to enable us to relive that time, and I was backstage.

L) "Backstage at the Fillmore?"

A) It was more than just the Fillmore because I covered other things as well. I was at the Isle of Wight. I was on the staff at Woodstock, at Tanglewood when they first introduced rock concerts during the summer, Newport Rock Festival, all over the East Coast. During that period, I never got to California so I never saw the original Fillmore West or the big concerts out there.

L) When you were talking before you said that there were a bunch of filmmakers hanging out at the Fillmore. Was it because of its proximity to NYU and all the graduate students?

A) I'd say ninety-nine and a half percent of the staff at the Fillmore was NYU students or NYU dropouts. The whole technical staff of the theater was NYU people, partly because of its proximity and also because there were so many good people there. People continually ask me, "How come the music business? That just doesn't gel with my image of you." I understand that because it's true. I was there for several reasons. I did love and still love the music from that period, though not all of it. There were groups that came, and I just put ear plugs in. I couldn't bear them; they were disgusting. Groups like Mountain and Vanilla Fudge, just lots of rotten rock-and-roll groups.

L) Like everything else.

A) But I liked most of it. I hated the music scene. It was sexist and chauvinist, just revolting in its treatment of women, that is, the way the musicians and the business side of it operated. But the technical staff at the Fillmore was really a remarkable, dedicated group of people who were, of course, almost all men. They loved what they were doing for the challenge and excitement of the production. Whether it was producing music or live theater, it was the real excitement of running the theater that held those people. So there was an atmosphere of excitement and interest and people who liked what they were doing, and there was so much to learn; it was fascinating to me.

L) But it was not a filmmaking scene, officially.

A) It wasn't the filmmaking scene, but lots of filmmakers from NYU, students, were involved in one way or another on the technical staff because the rock-and-roll business was the exciting field to be connected with. People like Jonathan Kaplan, Alan Arkush, the playwright John Ford Noonan. It gave you wide experience with things that had an energy all their own. Of course, very shortly movies began to be made about it. Because I was there, I knew how to do it. On the night they were shooting *Mad Dogs and Englishmen,* or whatever, they'd always need an extra magazine loader, and I'd pick up a few dollars and do that. I was able to hang around and absorb other things as well. I always figured that rock and roll would be my backdoor to the film business.

L) But it wasn't?

A) It was in a funny way; it was and it wasn't. I started hanging out in the Fillmore during the spring of my first year at NYU Film School, the spring of 1968, when it opened. Then I got hired on staff in August of 1968.

L) Were you the only woman on technical?

A) No. I was employed by the light show, the staff of which was hired by Bill Graham, so I wasn't on the actual payroll of the Fillmore. The light show was on the Fillmore staff. I was part of the light show, and there were other women in the light show. As far as the technical staff in the Fillmore itself, there were women who handled the concessions, the ushers, and things like that, but were not true technical staff, not until sometime late into the second year. A remarkable woman named Candice Brightman was then hired as the lighting designer. She had started off working as an assistant. She was the only woman on the staff in a full professional capacity.

L) It's interesting about lighting. As a photographer and in film school, you understood the importance of lighting. Working at Fillmore, did you get a chance to work with the light itself?

A) I didn't, but I watched it. I was exposed to all of this, including the twenty-four-track recording sessions that they operated out of there for the live albums, and then there was a lot of video that was done. It was an absolutely invaluable technical learning experience in all facets, all related to film in one way or another, whether you would think so or not, and I say that it was my backdoor to film, even though I'd already made my first film, *May Wilson*, and was starting on several other films. I was earning money and had a big break with John Lennon and Yoko Ono, which enabled me to buy my Steenbeck, which is what (though not the way I originally imagined it should be) set me on my feet. That still remains the single most important piece of equipment, object, thing, that I own. It gave me the freedom to work, having that piece of equipment, and I had wanted one for years. This goes back to your original question. I always knew what I wanted; the question was how to get it, and I got it. At that point, I owned an editing bench, rewinds, synchronizer and splicer, and trimmer, all of which I'd picked up at auction. Also, the Fillmore is where I met my husband, who was the sound engineer; he designed and built and ran the whole sound system there.

L) So you knew him for a long time.

A) He did the mix on *May Wilson*. That's when we first got to know each other well, and he did the mix and audio on my three subsequent films.

L) I love *It Happens to Us*. I still look at it today. I think it needs to be shown on television now. It needs more exposure.

A) I always wanted my equipment and a place to work, and the first loft that I had was above the Fillmore. John and I split it; he had the front half with his workbench and operation, and I had the rear, a screening room and cutting room.

L) And you could hear the floor rocking?

A) No, it was well insulated! Anyhow, it was in those offices that we had the first International Festival of Women's Films screening committee meetings twice a week to look at the films to select for the festival.

L) Did you organize that or were you part of the group?

A) Christina Nordstrom organized the festival, but the whole thing was born at the 1971 Flaherty Film Seminar, which is where Julia Reichert, Jim Klein, and I met, and New Day Films was born out of that, also.

L) They had a hell of time distributing *Growing Up Female.*

A) They had just started out on their own.

L) They had a terrible time getting it seen as I recall.

A) Yes, and that seminar was very important, seminal for many of us. The seminar was programmed by Willard Van Dyke, who brought us all together. History was made at that Flaherty Seminar because New Day came out of it and the first International Festival of Women's Films came out of it.

L) What was the Arzner retrospective? Was that the first? Did you have something to do with setting that up, because no one had ever really looked at her work.

A) Yes, it all came out of that group of people. I was not personally responsible for that.

L) Were there any women film directors whose work you were aware of when you were in the formative stages, those whom you were particularly interested in, or, now, for that matter?

A) The only two people who I knew existed were Shirley Clarke and Agnes Varda, but I wouldn't say their work at the time was influential, because I hadn't seen it. It wasn't something that I specifically admired but I knew they existed and that was important.

L) You're associated in the criticism that I've read with almost inventing or perfecting the personal, autobiographical woman's film, having given it its fullest expression, almost defining a genre that feminists have claimed as feminist. I want to know how you feel about that, but I also want to know who did you look to? Were there models for you? From whom did you learn?

A) I don't know. I can't say that there was a specific filmmaker I admired and imitated, but I've seen so many films that through osmosis I've assimilated many people's work. But I wouldn't credit myself with defining a genre.

L) Because certainly the traditional documentarists had not given you anything.

A) How I work (and have always worked) came out of just the only way I've known how to be and do. It has never occurred to me to do things any differently. I did what came out of me. I don't know. There is no way to know when you see a lot of things how you are absorbing them and what you're taking from one thing and combining with what you've taken from another and how that's all percolating around in there and gelling in some way. The movies that I admired most and the film directors who were my "heroes" (I've never had any real heroes), whose work I loved, were the following. I would go to see every film that Ingmar Bergman ever made, and Truffaut, Kurosawa, Alain Resnais, the classic European, foreign directors of the 1960s. Antonioni. Those were my favorite directors during the years that I fell in love with cinema.

L) But you certainly did not model yourself on them.

A) No, that's what I'm trying to tell you. I had no specific models, and I didn't know any documentary works.

L) I'm wondering, maybe the visual arts influences had an impact. To be able to tell yourself that it was okay, somehow say to yourself, "Yes, I can do this personal investigation on film; I can deal with my personal concerns."

A) And none of that is anything I can articulate from that perspective; I can't explain it to you.

L) You have to give yourself permission to do that. Some place you have to say to yourself, "It's okay to take this risk." It's such a personal thing. Visual artists do it. All paintings are self-portraits in some way. I'm just guessing. Maybe because of your mother and the artists that you knew, and the fact that you felt that you were an artist, you were able to transfer that, to make a little shift to one side, and say, "Yes, I can do this on film."

A) I don't know because the first ambition I ever had when I was eleven years old was to be a writer. That's what I was going to be when I grew up.

L) Did you keep a diary?

A) No, I began to write a novel when I was eleven years old. I don't think this story has ever been published, and I've never talked about this before in this situation. My consciousness was reminded of this, and I finally saw it in the right perspective about five years ago. It finally connected. I think it is significant—I think it's very significant—and I hadn't ever understood it in that way until that particular time, the story of my abandoned novel when I was eleven years old, and what it reveals about the consistently warring sides of my creative impulses, whatever they are. This sounds terribly pretentious. I don't mean it to be. The story is the following: I began this novel, and I was always an extremely romantic person, drawn back to pioneer days. I loved the Indians; I loved horses. All my life, I've really wanted to live in an age that depends on the horse. I always felt I was born a hundred years after I should have been. Of course, knowing now what I know about how women were treated in those days, who knows what things might have been like? In any event, this novel was set in the Northwest, about a pioneer woman who was a great horsewoman, who lived in the woods, and whose life combined the intersecting of the white wilderness pioneers and the Indians. It was full of romance, adventure, and love—all these things that were part of my eleven-year-old's fantasy life. However, after I had written a couple of chapters, I got to a point where I first introduced the Indians. I had already built up in my mind all kinds of images of what the Indian lore and culture was in the part of the country where I had the physical setting for my film, which was in the woods in the Northwest.

L) You called it a film.

A) I did? My novel. I wanted it to be accurate. So, I went to the library to do research on the lifestyle and culture of the Northwest Indians who actually, historically, resided in the part of the country where the location was for the setting of my book. When I did this, I found that the Northwest Indians were totally, completely, diametrically opposite to my fantasies of what that Indian culture was all about. What I had done was to transpose Plains Indians to that locale. The actual Northwest Indians were sedentary. They fished, they farmed, they didn't use horses, and they didn't fit at all into the story that I wanted to write. I was completely thrown off course by this, confused, and did not know how to handle it or what to do. Consequently, I abandoned the book, which for years gave me terrible feelings of guilt that I was a quitter, and that I would never finish anything that I began, that I was a failure. I abandoned it because I was never able to reconcile my fantasy with the reality. I could not bring myself to go ahead and write the book the way I wanted it to be, based on my fantasy, and make it completely false. I was unable to readjust and rewrite the story that I wanted, to accommodate the reality that I discovered, because of the accuracy that I expected of myself. I simply was unable to combine the two, and didn't know where to turn or how to proceed and so I just abandoned it. I couldn't readjust my fantasies, but I also could not go against what I had discovered was accurate.

L) So this is the tension between the creative, the imaginative artist, and the documentarist who said, "This is reality, these are the details that I want to capture."

A) Fiction and reality.

L) But you inadvertently called it a film. What about that? That's one of the questions that I was going to ask you. Do you have a feature film in your future? I mean, are you going to be making a dramatic or narrative film?

A) Probably.

L) Is that something you want to do? Because you're already so associated in the literature with the documentary tradition.

A) Well, that's a trap. It's also a difficulty that I have no response to, because of the very fact that this is the question everybody asks and this is the prejudice that is so deeply ingrained.

L) Well, it is a prejudice. It's true. It's true. It's a doubled-edged prejudice because ironically my perception is that women do best, so far anyway, as independent and often documentary filmmakers, and you exemplify that to a certain degree. You're a pioneer, and you're a leader in that area and that is seen almost as if it weren't a good choice. It's almost seen as if that's what women have to do, because they can't make it after all in the "real" film world.

A) I know, and I hate that.

L) I know, I do too. It's absolutely true that it's much harder for women to make it in Hollywood, whatever Hollywood means, even if they wanted to, so there's that awful fact staring at us. If you made a feature film or a fiction film, if you wrote your novel in film, would you do it independently?

A) Yes, but that's because I don't think I would have any choice in the matter. It's that or nothing.

L) Even with your credits, even with your training, even with your skill, you feel that way?

A) I'm nobody. I'm a documentary film-maker.

L) Aside from the fact that you may or may not want to make it in Hollywood, how do you get to be "somebody"?

A) Outside the system.

L) You get to be somebody outside the system? I'm thinking of people like Lee Grant, for example. She made a beautiful feature, *Tell Me a Riddle*. Did you see that?

A) Yes.

L) Can you never be validated? What the hell is this?

A) Well, the question is validated by whom? Whom are you talking about?

L) The people who give you the budgets of six million dollars.

A) Nobody gives it to you. They take a pound of flesh. Claudia Weill has been severely injured, for example.

L) Why do you say that?

A) I think a lot of things, and this would be a very long discussion, predicated on explaining the nature of the business. No offense intended, but from the way that you ask the question, there are certain things that you don't know.

A) I'm sure that there's a lot that I don't know about how things are financed, and who makes it. I'm aware of that structure. The question sounds naive simply because I want you to talk about it, but yes, there's a lot I don't know. But it seems to me that—in the way a visual artist wants to be collected by the Whitney or by the Museum of Modern Art, whatever they may think of those institutions and however reprehensible one may think some of the administrations' policies are—a filmmaker must want to have a chance to make "a major feature," all in quotes. There has to be that ambition. If you're ambitious at all, you have to want to see if you can do it. And when they say you can't come into the Fillmore, the part of you that says, "Oh yes, I can," and makes you go out and get on staff, is the same part of you that is going to say, "God damn it, I can do that, too." I'm thinking to myself, okay, how's she going to do it?

A) Well, she hasn't figured all that out yet, but

never fear. I see a lot of possible ways of going about it, none of which involves doing it out in California to begin with. Claudia did it a right way. Her way was/is one of the best ways to do it. The question is then how you play it after you've gotten that first crack, in order to retain your integrity and your control over your work, and not allow them to take you over because you want that so badly that you'll sell your soul, or make compromises that backfire on you.

L) That's right.

A) Famous last words; come back in twenty years and see where we're at, but I hope I won't sell my soul, and it may mean that there are certain things that I might be able to do that I won't ever get to do. I don't know. I'm looking forward to seeing Martha Coolidge's new film. It's taken her almost ten years to do it. She's got a major feature coming out called *Valley Girl.* I've heard mixed things about it, and I'm curious to see it. But I know what she's gone through, and I know what I think of some of that, and I know why I've made some of the choices that I've made to do things differently. I may or may not end up succeeding professionally at that same level, and if I don't, it would be inaccurate for me to say that there won't be part of me that might be sorry about it. But if I don't it's because I've made other choices in my life for other things I consider equally valuable that I want to have, do, and experience, that may not be as important as sacrificing everything to make it in Hollywood. You know the danger in talking this way is that people will say "sour grapes," but there really are other choices one can make about life that can be as satisfying as a certain kind of American definition of career success.

L) I'm thinking of women like Joan Micklin Silver. She made *Hester Street,* but I'm not sure what else after that.

A) Oh, yes, she's done a number of things: *Between the Lines, Head Over Heels.* None of them has been as successful commercially. But the thing that you musn't overlook is that she made *Hester Street* with family money. Her husband is a very wealthy real estate investor. They financed and bankrolled their own work. If you have deep personal resources, enough financial backing, you can do anything. This is how things work in capitalist America, and I'm a beneficiary of this system as well and am aware of the fact that I'm privileged and have also been lucky. Joan is doing well. She's continuing to work. She directed *Bernice Bobs Her Hair.* She's accomplished, and she's hard working, and doing well. I would say for my own tastes, there's only one woman director, internationally, whose work I admire as the most important director, who's developing a coherent and compelling body of work that's world-class, that I consider as significant creatively in the history of the medium as Ingmar Bergman, and that is Margarethe Von Trotta, the German director. This country hasn't produced anybody of that stature yet. I'm trying to think of which woman has, first of all, even been able to make enough films in the U.S. to create a body of work to evaluate.

L) Yes. Having the body of work.

A) But then Von Trotta has only done a few films.

L) Well, she splits credits on *Lost Honor* with Von Schlondorff.

A) I've seen five of her films so far, *The Second Awakening of Christa Klages, The Lost Honor of Katerina Blum, Sisters, Sheer Madness,* and *Marianne and Julianne.*

L) Let's return to you now. You taught at NYU. In production? Documentary?

A) I taught narrative production for two years, which was absurd. But that was the opening, that's what they asked me to teach, and that's what I did. I've always felt uncomfortable about that because I didn't feel qualified to do it. I've yet to make my first narrative film.

L) Well, you have written a novel.

A) My unfinished preadolescent novel—it doesn't count.

L) You should go back and make it into a film.

A) Talking about my NYU teaching experience—I felt that I learned more than my students did. It was a unique and fabulous opportunity for me. I knew enough basics about the filmmaking process that are accurate for both narrative and documentary productions. I was able to be an effective and a good teacher even though I hadn't made any narrative films because of the nature of the program at NYU and what kinds of things the kids needed to be exposed to. I found I was pretty good as a nuts-and-bolts critic when it came to looking at scripts and works-in-progress and those kinds of things. They transcend specific training. You have a certain sensibility in the basics, knowledge. It worked out okay.

L) But you're not affiliated with them any more?

A) No, I did that for two years. I resigned because it took up too much of my time, and I was starting to be in production full time again. I just could not make my own films and teach.

L) A lot of teachers have this dilemma, especially in the arts, the visual arts. They find that they're giving so much to the students and preparing for the classes, dealing with the materials that come in from the class, that they don't have any time left to do their own work. It becomes agonizing. Do you think you'd like to go back and do that again sometime?

A) Yes, I'd like to teach at some other point in my life, but it'll probably be at a point when I'm out of production. I can't see combining the two now because it requires you to be available several days a week, every week on an academic schedule. That means you can't go out of town.

L) Do you want to say anything about the new production? Are you ready to talk about it?

A) There's not much to say. It's about Richard Haas and architecture, architectural preservation, and trompe-l'oeil painting. There's an article in today's *New York Times* about his newest work, the dedication of which I'm shooting next Thursday.

L) How did you become interested in him?

A) I've just seen his work and have always liked it. I slowly came to know that it was all the work of the same person I was consistently attracted to. I spent a lot of time in Italy last year and found that this same kind of work flourished originally in the sixteenth century there. It goes all the way back to the days of Pompeii and I'd come across it before in Italy and liked it a lot. I began to think about a project that would permit me to explore the Italian illusionist tradition and Haas's modern application of these techniques. I also realized that he had to know about the Italian work and that it had to have been a major influence. When I was in Florence this past December [1982] I saw a book of his work in a bookshop. Then it all fell into place. I knew this was something I'd like to do. I had a grant from the Architectural Division of the National Endowment for the Arts for a slightly different project that was four years old and no longer of interest to me. I got permission to go ahead with the new idea, looked his name up in the phone book and called him, and now I'm doing it.

L) Let's talk about feminism.

A) It's not a "feminist" film.

L & A) I don't know what that means.

L) Well, I don't know what that means anymore either.

A) I've optioned a novel for possible future use. I don't know yet whether I'll ever end up making that film, but I've got somebody working on it.

L) If you're a feminist, if you're a woman, and you've been through what we've been through, what you've been through as a filmmaker and as a woman director, you can look at a certain subject or any subject matter, given all that experience, and still have a feminist film, even though it may not be about women. There's a certain perspective that you bring to things. That's my opinion. The subject matter doesn't have to be female in order to be feminist. It's the point of view, the perspective, the person doing it, the methodology. Women have to talk about men sometimes. That shouldn't be a taboo subject. But it's how you do it. Do you do it as a peer? This is an equal, this is another human being, this is an artist whose work I respect, and you hope to be treated in the same way. Is there anything that I haven't asked you that you feel like talking about?

A) Well, there are lots of things, and I can't think about them all now. In this kind of process, I really need to have the right buttons pushed to be brought out. I could talk to you for ten hours and we still wouldn't cover everything.

CHRONOLOGY

*M*EG *S*WITZGABLE

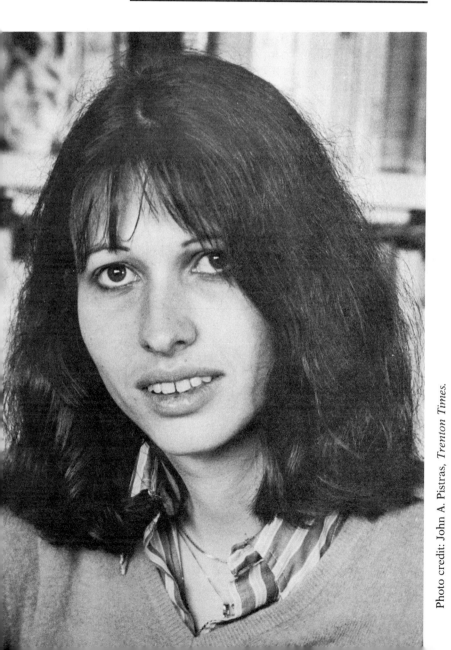

Meg Switzgable

Meg Switzgable is president of Foresight Films, a nonprofit, tax-exempt group that was formed to distribute films of social significance on subjects not previously scrutinized. She produced and directed the Academy Award- and Emmy Award-nominated film *In Our Water*, which she is currently distributing. She has spent the past year writing *Passing thru Linden*, a mystery/love story set in America's industrial heartland. She is presently gathering production funds, scouting locations, and completing the development for this film, which is set for production in fall 1987.

Born February 16, 1955, Meg Switzgable graduated with a B.F.A. from Boston University and now lives in Brooklyn, New York.

Stills from *In Our Water*. Left: Toxic chemicals dumped in neighboring landfill leach into ground water contaminating the well of Frank and Rita Kaler. Photo credit: Frank Kaler. Right: Frank and Rita Kaler examine drinking water from their well as it turns brown with toxic chemicals. Photo credit: Paul Eric Felder.

INTERVIEW

Interview on November 29, 1982, with Meg Switzgable, director of *In Our Water* and *Passing thru Linden.*

L) I thought you had gone to Princeton University.

M) I started out there; I graduated from Boston University.

L) When did you decide to go into film?

M) I was always interested in film, but I never majored in it. I got involved after I got out of school. Acutally, one summer I'd done filming, when I was a sophomore in college, at the NYU summer program, that intensive program where you make about eight films, but other than that . . .

L) You were working in sixteen mm?

M) Sixteen mm.

L) With whom did you study at NYU?

M) Haig Menujian and Charles Merrill did the program that summer; that was about ten years ago.

L) Were they good?

M) They were both good. One of them, the one that died, was really the creative force behind that whole film department; I don't know if they're still there.

L) So you took an intensive summer course at NYU. Were there any other women in your class?

M) There was the woman who cut my film. What they did was put together crews of four people. There were Mona, this other woman, and I—I don't know what happened to her. There were a few women in the class as I remember. I don't know; I don't clearly remember; but the guy in our group went a little crazy after the first film. He made it through the first film and left, so there were basically three women, and we rotated jobs.

L) He actually left school?

M) Well, I don't know what happened to him, he couldn't handle it.

L) Because you were all women?

M) I don't know; I'm sure he had other problems. I don't think it had anything to do with that.

L) What did you major in at college?

M) I was a sculptor.

L) That's very interesting, because I come to my interest in film through the arts. I found very little information on women directors, very little.

M) That's because there are so few women.

L) There are a few but even the ones there are . . .

M) In the independent community, there are a lot, but when you get to features there are very few.

L) There is a definite crossover between art

and film, sculpture especially. It's always been my contention . . .

M) . . . and dance. I had nine years of dance, when I was much younger, and I think that influenced me.

L) That's wonderful, because they're all things that combine viewing with space and time.

M) Well, that's how I initially became interested in film, it wasn't in documentary films. I wasn't socially conscious at all. I came totally out of the arts.

L) When did you decide you wanted to be an artist? Obviously, you knew you wanted to be an artist.

M) At three, I wanted to be a dancer. From that point on, I stayed in the arts. I can remember consciously wanting to be a dancer first. But then I went through the stage of not wanting to do this. I was seventeen.

L) You went into the visual arts in college or had you started that before?

M) Way before. Since I was a child I remember being interested in the arts.

L) But never specifically film or video?

M) I think my interest in film came about in college.

L) So you were taking that course at NYU and it was good. What kind of piece did you make?

M) Each of us made six or seven short films.

Then we worked on the films of the other people in the crews; we rotated.

L) I have a master's degree in theater, and that is similar to when I was studying directing. We took turns acting, stage managing, and doing lighting for each other's plays.

M) Right. We rotated. That's how it works. But, you know, it was sixteen millimeter, small. There was no synch sound.

L) Everything was mixed later.

M) We jut didn't use synch cameras; they were Bolexes or something.

L) Really? Sixteen?

M) Yes.

L) I know about the Bolex eight, but I didn't know about sixteen.

M) Well, they're the old ones with turrets. But it was fun, anyway, that's how I met Mona.

L) What's Mona's last name?

M) Mona Davis. She's an editor, and when I got the money to put this film together, I called her.

L) So there you were, you had worked on other people's films in industry, it said in an interview I read in *Sightlines*.

M) I had been doing commercial films, industrial films.

L) But you got experience with the technology.

M) Yes. Actually, I was interested in experimental films; I never really thought that I would be doing a documentary.

L) So that experimental films were the kinds of things that you had made in the class?

M) No, but that's what I had an interest in, read about, went to see.

L) Whose work did you see?

M) Maya Deren, Stan Brackage, that whole tradition.

L) What made you think you could be a filmmaker? How did you start conceiving of yourself as a filmmaker? I'm interested in the inner transition that made you leap from dance and sculpture into film.

M) First of all, I couldn't make a statement through sculpture or tell a story; it was still, it wasn't in motion. There are certain aesthetic things that I think made me want to go into film to express certain things. Then I didn't know how I was going to make them or get the money to do it; it seemed totally unreachable. It was also mechanical, which sculpture isn't. It is to a degree, but you can do it by yourself, you don't have to do it with a crew.

L) There's something about coordinating the technology that, what? Does it act as a barrier?

M) I think it does, initially. You want to do it, but you don't know how to go about doing it and getting the information and how to raise the money to do it.

L) The money is the big thing.

M) The money, yes. It's so much money and you wonder, God, how am I going to get that money?

L) How did you get the money?

M) I wrote a proposal. In raising money, if you can get just a little bit of money, then it helps get the project off the ground. Other people are then willing to put money in. It took me about six months to raise the first $80,000 on it, and really what pulled in that initial $80,000 was a grant from the Fund for New Jersey. Do you know the director there?

L) No. It used to be Gordon McGinnis.

M) Gordon, yes. He left to work on Dick Leone's campaign.

L) But before we get into *In Our Water*, I'm still interested in a little place there that interests me, a transition.

M) I'm in transition right now, starting to get a spell of, God, how did I do this last one? How can I start this next film?

L) Don't think about it.

M) You're only as good as you film. When you're in the middle of it, and you're in the process, it all seems to be working, even though there may be complications. When you start again, the blank sheet is what you face.

L) It's similar to when you've stopped running for a couple of weeks and you have to get out there on the road again. "Oh no, how can I get the energy to do this?"

M) Right.

L) After you had graduated from college, you got a job in commercial film?

M) Not immediately. I worked for a still photographer for a while. I even got pushed into modeling for money, which I immediately got out of. I got the modeling job through the photographer, and ended up in front of the camera; the money was good.

L) Have you studied photography, too?

M) Yes, still photography. I did a lot of still photography when I first got out of school.

L) Do you think that background helps to get into film?

M) I don't know. I guess it must all help. An art background is good in terms of composition and lighting and space and sensibility.

L) I think so.

M) I was working for a still photographer and then I left. I got into modeling for a while, which was horrible.

L) Many a little girl dreams of it. Well, I did, and was told I'm not tall enough, that I'd never be able to model anything except children's clothes. Everybody wants to be a model.

M) You did? I didn't. It's not glamorous, it's disgusting.

L) Did you encounter sexism?

M) *Oh yes!* But that's the nature of the business, and if you're in it, then you know that. So I decided not to pursue it, and shortly after that, I got a job with a film company in Princeton.

    L) Which one?

    M) Calquest.

    L) I don't know it.

    M) That was an odd situation. I worked there for about a year, and then when I got the money to do this film, it was difficult. It was just a tough situation.

    L) A lot of employers, whether they're men or women, think of their employees as belonging to them.

    M) Right.

    L) And anything that they think up while they're employed belongs to the employers?

    M) No, they didn't think that; they understood that this was something that I was doing outside the job. They understood that, but it was just very hard. The role reversal was very difficult for them. Here I was working for them, and then they were going to be working for me on the new project. Even though they accepted it, they really didn't accept it, and that's where the problem arose.

    L) You were apprenticing in the film industry, basically, and you got the idea for *In Our Water*.

    M) Actually, I had the idea even before I

started working for them and just did research from that period, on my own.

L) You're from that area, so you know what goes on in New Jersey. You were born and raised in New Jersey?

M) Yes. My father had bladder cancer, and he suspected that it was environmentally induced. He collects information on different subjects. I said I was interested in doing a film on the nuclear waste problems and he said, "No, do the chemical waste problem." This was way before Love Canal had happened or anything had been in the news. There was hardly anything in the press; maybe once every six months you'd see a little story on the back page. He gave me several books and a file of clippings that he'd kept, and I was just outraged at all that was going on. I think that's what spurred me on.

L) A commitment. You can feel it in the film, that you do have an ax to grind. I think that that makes it wonderful for people like me, and makes it somewhat irritating to some other people who feel, she's got a point of view here, she's really advocating something. It's an advocacy film. It's by no means an objective treatment.

M) I don't believe in objective films though. I believe that you have to tell a story, and if you're going to tell a story, it has to have a point of view. If you're not telling a story, then okay.

L) In a sense, you're a character in the film really. Not appearing in front of the camera, but no one could possibly miss your commitment and your sense of outrage, which comes through as energy. To spend four years on that project, you had to have had strong feelings.

M) Yes.

L) I responded to that immediately. The film was popular at Rutgers even before we bought it, and from the minute it got there, it's been booked solid. It's used. There's been interest in the film all along. People who share your point of view love the sensibility. But some South Brunswick officials and other people who work regularly with the Department of Environmental Protection kept saying that they wished it had been different. That's their problem, though.

M) You know the sequence when we got into Jerry English's office? All of a sudden Frank decided he was going to go there. I did a screening in Atlantic City and a man came up from the Associated Press and introduced himself. He said he had been there that day with the man from "60 Minutes" and they had gone crazy. They were trying to come up with ways of burning the film. He said lower management was applauding us on, and that the upper management was going crazy. They were trying to get this man from the Associated Press and "60 Minutes" out of there so they wouldn't see what was going on. And the man from "60 Minutes" wanted to get in on the action. I thought it was so funny.

L) It was an interesting scene with the secretary.

M) She was there because they had an interview with her that day.

L) The secretary or Jerry English?

M) Jerry English.

L) I thought that the secretary was very interesting.

M) I think that disturbed them a lot, that one sequence.

L) She handled it well. Given her role and her position, I think she did the right thing, but she comes out looking somewhat intransigent. It was a very interesting sequence.

M) But I hope it does rattle them a bit. Although they don't like it, I am pleased they at least react to it.

L) You know that South Brunswick had a toxic waste fair one weekend? I went and they screened the film all day long. I thought you were going to be there, but you weren't, and I met Frank. The officials were all sitting at their booths at the fair saying, "Meg Switzgable makes South Brunswick look bad." I said, "No, no, she made South Brunswick look good, she pushed you to do this, what you're doing." Every department now—the fire department, the police department—has become toxic waste conscious. They have a toxic waste task force in the fire department. South Brunswick is one of the few towns in New Jersey that does. You really pushed them to be aware of this. Now they're probably light years ahead of other communities in the sensitivity toward it, so it's been good for South Brunswick. But officials are grumbling, "Who's gonna buy a house in South Brunswick after they see that film?"

M) It's not just South Brunswick, it's everywhere.

L) Have you stayed with the story down the road?

M) The Kalers have become like family.

L) How are they? I asked Frank how his daughter was, because I felt as if I knew him, and he was so congenial.

M) He's so eloquent, too. Finding him was really great because he's such a good speaker that it was easy to get a lot of information.

L) You had the idea for the film before you met Frank.

M) Before I met Frank, yes.

L) How did you find him?

M) I just poked around for stories.

L) What happened to that land fill operation?

M) It's closed down.

L) It's still in the phone book.

M) I guess they still have an operation there. I'm told that they might even be able to reopen because, as you know, there's no place to put the waste. They have a tendency to allow some of these places to reopen. I'm not really up to date on how far the contamination has spread or whose well has now shown contamination. It's definitely traveling. I don't know who in the path of that contamination has got bad water now.

L) New Jersey's set up in such a way that every town controls its own waste disposal. They are like little medieval dukedoms or something. And there's nobody that's working regionally to solve the problem, so I don't know what's going on with my town.

M) Where does your water supply come from in North Brunswick?

L) I think it comes from a reservoir, or . . .

M) I wouldn't drink it. I think Princeton's water is bad. When I'm in New Jersey, in Princeton, my hair feels greasy, it doesn't quite get washed, and my skin gets sort of dried out and itchy. It's probably bad water.

L) Let me just ask you some questions about being a woman. Did you have any role models? You had mentioned Maya Deren.

M) Well, I didn't really have her as a role model, because my film is so different.

L) You decided to make a documentary because of your father, more or less, and you got interested in this issue?

M) I learned a lot in the process of making it. I didn't want to make a film with a narrator telling you what was going on. I wanted the viewer to experience what the people were going through in the process of confronting this problem, and develop it in a story form so that it had dramatic development and that it wasn't just information. I think this subject tends to be technical. Sometimes people are overwhelmed either with the horror or their inability to comprehend the factual material involved, like, what are the chemicals in the water, the hydrology, the geology, and everything that causes this problem. I tried to put it into very simple terms so that people could understand what the problem was and how they might be affected by it, or how they could do something about it if they were affected by it.

L) I think that worked, because you identify so strongly with the Kalers.

M) I tried to make it human. It was an interesting experience because I had never really been very political or environmentally conscious before this. I'd met environmentalists, but I never thought much about something that was affecting not just trees and animals. It was a concern that never really got me angry or upset. There were people who were involved in it. It was the total disregard for people's lives that caught me.

L) In making this film, getting to watch the whole process, did that get rid of your anger, having taken that action and done something with it? Did it discharge those feelings?

M) No, it never did. The problem's much worse now with the Reagan Administration's environmental policies. Certainly the problem has not gotten any better. What happens is that you become numb to it when you hear just one awful thing after another. You become numb and then if you get away from it and hear another story, you get angry again. It's important in the process to be moved by what you're filming.

L) Yes, I think so. It keeps the commitment going. What kinds of problems did you encounter (I'll assume that you did) during the process of making the film? Maybe because you were young, or because you're a woman or anything like that, or did you not?

M) Well, not really. Sometimes it helped being a young woman. Some of the interviews and material I was able to get was because I was young and a woman. They were unsuspecting of information that I have and became very angry with the questions that I asked. For instance, the EPA official that we had in the film—I had warned him beforehand I had some really tough questions that I was going to ask him. He was from Princeton, and we had this very nice conversation. He was very sweet until I started interviewing him. Then his eyes kept darting back and forth, and he seemed a little bit nervous; I didn't realize how nervous he was. You usually have release forms that you have people sign before the interview. Mona, who was working as my associate producer and manager of production, had forgotten to get this paper signed beforehand, so she went back to ask him sign it after the interview. He was in the corner, crazed, totally crazed. I somehow convinced him to sign it, and said we would continue with the interview; that's when we got the last question which was used in the film. I found that if you ask bureaucrats technical questions, they can get around them by lying. The man whom I asked about how the people would be affected gave this spiel about their tightening the regulations and so forth. He gave a bureaucratic spew of information.

It's the simple questions that I found they couldn't answer: What about human lives? What about notifying the people involved? To this day, there is *no one* who has the job to notify these people. It was the really simple, basic questions that we couldn't get answers to.

L) Absolutely not. I also found that when I met with county officials at the Toxic Waste Fair. County officials were very nice and friendly until I asked them whom I would go to if I found a problem. "Are you responsible?" "Well, no, it's not our responsibility." Nothing is their responsibility. They just don't want to take it on.

M) I guess that that was an advantage, I don't know. I mean, I didn't realize that until afterwards, but . . .

L) That's good, that's good. What about the fund-raising and the technology part? How did you get all the equipment? Did you have to buy it? Rent it?

M) Well, usually when you hire a cameraman or a sound man, he has his own equipment. I bought an editing machine, and we acquired some equipment along the way, but you don't have to have a camera. Most people don't even have editing machines. When you hire a cameraperson, they usually have all their own equipment. And I married my cameraman from *In Our Water*.

L) Oh! After? Before? During?

M) After.

L) So, you hired this guy for the film?

M) This is a funny story. I had known him before; I had met him at NYU. In fact, Mona and I both liked him. He was cute; he ran the office and the equipment and was a couple of years older, and then Mona recommended him when I was looking for a cameraman. He came and we remembered each other. He was actually working on a feature at that time, so I hired his partner. A couple of months later we met and hit it off.

L) That's nice. Did it affect your working relationship?

M) Not really. He didn't get involved with the production of the film at all; when he did shoot, he'd just come in for one day and work. We have a tendency to fight.

L) That's interesting.

M) He's a very good cameraman, and I'm going to work with him more on the next film. He really wasn't that involved.

L) But, when you're the director, what does it mean to be the director in terms of working with a technical crew? You have to understand how the technology works so that you can direct that.

M) Right.

L) Even though you don't necessarily own it, the equipment itself, you have to understand everything about it.

M) Right, right.

L) Did you have a storyboard for the film?

M) Well, it is a documentary; it's not a dramatic film. I knew that I wanted the film to center on Frank, and I wanted it to develop over a period of time. I had an idea of what might happen, but with a documentary, you can only control it to a certain degree, especially if you're not using narration. I knew I wanted it to develop in time, and that I wanted it to center on Frank and Teddy when they lived alongside the landfill. I had a story; I actually wrote a script, but I didn't hold to it when I went into shooting. It's good to have a definite idea of what you want before you go into the situation to shoot. You can thereby control the lighting and the situation a little bit more, but you can't script it exactly.

L) So you had a lot of postproduction work?

M) Yes. There's only a limited degree to which you can make those kinds of changes in the editing.

L) How many hours of film did you shoot?

M) About 35 hours of film, about 35.

L) What did you do with all the outtakes?

M) We kept them.

L) That's good. Fund-raising. You got an initial grant from the Fund for New Jersey, which enabled you to get started and then . . .

M) Well, within a month, I got $80,000, but they gave me the first ten. Then I worked through that money and realized the problem was getting worse, that we had to raise more money to continue to film, so I stopped about a year into it to raise another $80,000. Finally I raised a little bit at the end, about $40,000.

L) Do you work full-time at something else?

M) Not during the production of it I didn't.

L) That's tough. Did you pay yourself a salary?

M) A little bit, it's not much, and I haven't paid myself any money for the last couple of years, which is not the best position to be in, but . . . you sort of make it.

L) What's your current project? You said you're working on something now?

M) I'm working on two ideas. One's a dramatic film that takes place in Elizabeth and Newark. I'm trying to develop a dramatic storyline that parallels what's going on in the environment, but isn't necessarily a story about discovery of pollution. It deals with the destruction of the environment on another level. What has always fascinated me about that whole area is that you have industry, the New Jersey Turnpike, and the airport all converging there. Even before I started this film, I'd always been drawn to that image on the Turnpike. You must know it—off Exit 13 where they have the Exxon Refinery. There's quite a large community beyond, behind there, affected by that pollution, but the story won't deal necessarily with the uncovering of someone being victimized. But it might on another level; that's what I'm working on.

L) It's important. My family is from Elizabeth. Both parents were born and raised in Elizabeth.

Both my mother and my aunt, her sister, died of cancer fairly young, and I often think about what kind of stuff lies percolating in there, when they were little, before they could even understand, just growing up in Elizabeth, breathing that stuff.

M) Right.

L) And it make me nervous.

M) What part of Elizabeth were they from?

L) My grandparents moved there, maybe after they got married. My maternal grandparents had a house on Magee Street, I think.

M) These industries provided the community with jobs and taxes, you know; they put the communities into existence. Now they're killing them off. I was in Manville, where the Johns-Manville plant is located. There are about thirty or forty people whom I met, all of whom had either asbestosis or mesothelioma. Not only did they have it, but practically all the people in their families had it, including those who never even worked in the plant.

L) It gets home on the clothing and gets into the air. It's scary.

M) And really what's happening is that this industry gave the town life, now it's taking it away. That's basically the story that I'd like to deal with, but through another element.

L) It sounds exciting. Are you in production now?

M) Oh, no. First of all, it's going to be a whole different type of fund-raising because it's dramatic.

I don't know if I can get foundation money for that, and it's going to cost a lot more. I have to develop a script, so I'm in the process of just starting it. The other film is on the Palestinian problem, and I'm just doing research on that now.

L) Over there?

M) No, I'm doing the research here. I want to base it on an American-Palestinian woman who is here in the United States, but deal with what has happened to the Palestinians, going back in the generations, maybe to their grandparents; 1948.

L) That's interesting, too. That one would probably get more funding.

M) Not necessarily. That one's also touchy. But it's very interesting and totally new to me. In a way it's more interesting. I know a lot about the other issue, and because of that I can deal with it in a more removed aesthetic kind of way, whereas the Palestinian issue is not like that, so I deal with it in a more immediate way.

L) How did you get interested in the Palestinian issue? I understand now how you got into the environment.

M) Well, my husband Bob was shooting a documentary over there two or three years ago. It was a film about the effects of the war on the children of the Middle East. He was in Israel, Lebanon, Syria, Egypt, Ethiopia.

L) What's the film called?

M) I can't remember the name of it. The director was English; that's where my first interest came from. What he was telling me was happening on the West Bank was totally different than what I'd been reading or ever supposed was happening there. It led me to do some further research, and it really shocked me, what's been going on there. But he was there. They had interviewed several of the mayors who have been removed from office. The week before he came back he had been interviewing the man whose legs were later blown off. We got back here, turned on the television news and that was on. It was pretty scary. That's where my interest came from. That film was sympathetic to the Palestinian problem. It was by no means radical but when it opened in Washington, the Jewish Defense League threatened to bomb the theater. That's when I started thinking. Why is this so incredibly important?

L) There are a lot of American Jews who probably feel that Israel has gone too far.

M) At this point after the massacre, yes.

L) Even before, but especially now they're starting to ask questions. It's interesting that in this country we don't get one view about it. I think the Jewish Defense League is probably one extreme kind of faction. I don't think they characterize the entire American Jewish response.

M) Oh, no, they're like the extreme groups in the PLO. They're definitely not typical. I wouldn't call them typical. They bombed a restaurant around here where I used to go to eat.

L) They bombed it?

M) Yes. This Lebanese restaurant.

L) Oh, for God's sake.

M) Killed a woman.

L) Oh, no. That's terrible. Let me change the subject now. Do you consider yourself a feminist, or part of the women's movement in any way?

M) I never was involved with any formal feminist movements, but I think I would consider myself a feminist. I guess the generation before me fought the battle, and continues to fight it. I've never been involved with any kind of movement. It's different for the generation before me, that was brought up in a different way than our generation. Probably the generation after mine will be brought up slightly different than we were.

L) For example, what would it be like for you without New Day for distribution?

M) Well, I don't like the idea. I think they've become less and less a feminist group. I don't like the idea of identifying myself with a feminist distribution group, just because it's feminist. To me, it's more the concern for a social issue, whether it be feminism or the environment or whatever. I don't like to identify myself with feminism in that way.

L) But how did you get involved with New Day?

M) It just seemed like a good group for distribution. It's a cooperative where you can be involved with the distribution, and they seemed like a really good group. I like the women involved. But I don't like the idea that it's "feminist." I think it's gotten away from that. I think that they should have men as well as women. You don't want to discriminate against the men.

L) Sounds like feminism means something negative and exclusive to you rather than . . .

M) Well, it does in some respects. I wasn't in the generation that fought for it; yet I did, but more on a personal level, I think. I wasn't brought up only to marry and have kids. I can't even imagine being brought up that way, but I'm sure the generation before me was, so it's a different thing that you're fighting against. I'm sure it's still out there; it's still something to fight against. But because I wasn't brought up in that kind of environment, it wasn't there to fight against, really.

L) I want to ask you if other than when you were working as a model for the photographer, whether you ever encountered what you would call "sexism" in your work.

M) I have, but when you work alone as a sculptor or a dancer, it's different. I'm sure if you work on a corporate level, you're going to find it. You notice it. Men definitely have a different attitude or sometimes feel more self-assured than women, in general. I haven't dealt with it in a way that's been totally incapacitating, though I'm aware that it exists, and I think women should continue to fight it. When you're sculpting, you're dealing with a piece of clay, by yourself. You do come in contact with it, I think, with other male directors. And obviously there must be a reason why there aren't too many women directors in Hollywood. There's obviously discrimination there, but I haven't personally yet been confronted with that.

L) Is it a goal of yours to do a feature?

M) I'd like to do a feature. I'd like this next film to be a feature-length dramatic film. I'm out of film, but I'm afraid of going through the system, so I'm trying to do it as an independent. And I don't think Hollywood would be interested anyway.

L) Why? You never know.

M) But I think even though you have less money working as an independent, you have more control over the product. Oh, I know where there's a problem. When you have men working for you, sometimes I've run into problems.

L) What kind?

M) Well, it's sometimes difficult for certain men to work under a woman. It depends on the personality.

L) In what way?

M) They're older than you, or the fact that you're a woman. There's a certain kind of resentment that I sometimes feel.

L) Did that happen with *In Our Water?*

M) Yes. Well, yes.

L) They were having trouble taking direction. I'm a woman boss, and the men who work for me don't seem to have that problem, I guess.

M) I think it depends on the man. It's not all men that have that problem. And I'm sure you run into it with certain women, too.

L) Those who would have trouble taking direction from another woman?

M) Yes. It just depends on the person, I think. You can't generalize.

L) But it does happen. And then what do you do? Do you fire the person?

L) You try to get out of the situation.

L) Is there a way to screen for that when you're interviewing people for positions?

M) I have a tendency to hire women over men; I just like to work with women better than men.

L) Well, that's a feminist position. I know what you mean.

M) I think you categorize me as a feminist, but I'm not . . .

L) More by birth than by training perhaps.

M) I appreciate what the women before me did, but I didn't come through it fighting. Do you know what I mean?

L) Yes, I do, I know what you mean. It's like it would be for my daughter, who's 21.

M) They sort of accept that they have these things.

L) And she doesn't think about having a problem as a woman.

M) That's because it hasn't hit her.

L) I was just thinking about your parents.

How do they feel about the film and your career, and your being a filmmaker? Are they supportive?

M) Yes, I guess so. My father's never seen the film. I don't get along with his wife, so there's been a controversy there, but I'm sure he's proud. And my mother enjoys the fact that it's made and out there.

L) It's done well in terms of critical response. I know there have been some articles. I read the piece in *Sightlines*. Has there been much written about it since the summer?

M) There have been a lot of articles all over, wherever it plays.

L) Has there been an in-depth review, or a journal article?

M) It's gotten a lot of reviews. Frank Mitchell did a piece on it in *The Nation*. I'd like it to be seen by more people.

L) In terms of your current work, the piece that you say you want to be a feature-length fiction piece. Tell me about your plans for that. How are you going to distribute it?

M) The first problem is to get the material down on paper so I can sell it, so I can get the money for it. It will be much easier to distribute a dramatic film.

L) Why do you think that? It seems that women who are documentarists have a lot of success, especially in getting their things on television. Has *In Our Water* been on TV?

M) No, we're holding off for a couple months.

It's best. Once you put it on TV, people have a tendency to tape it. Then you can't make the sales and rentals. Also, it builds up a reputation, and then they're more apt to want it. They want it now, but there's no money there, so I'm trying to find underwriting for it.

L) What kind? Whom do you mean?

M) When a show is put on TV, it is usually presented by or underwritten by Mobil or Exxon. Mobil or Exxon will never touch this. What they will do is pay the price of the show to have their name on the product.

L) They're the patrons.

M) Right.

L) That's interesting.

M) And then they'll usually put in advertising money because they want all the affiliate stations to pick it up at the same time. Documentaries have a very difficult time getting out. Not in the educational market, but in theaters; not so much in television, but in theaters. When you say documentary, people automatically assume that it's going to be an informational didactic piece of material. There's something about the word "documentary" that immediately turns people off, which I think is terrible.

L) They think, "I can see this in school; I don't have to pay to see this."

M) Right.

L) Has *In Our Water* been getting the bookings that you'd like?

M) We haven't done any solicitation yet in terms of doing mailings. Just on the reviews and what we've done, we seem to be getting a lot of interest in the film from libraries, community groups, small theaters, places that you'd never think would be interested.

L) Not necessarily in New Jersey?

M) Even abroad: Australia, New Zealand, Germany, Spain.

L) Well, that's because the film is aesthetically fine and is put together so well.

M) But even in the States, in small towns, in problem areas, in communities where they are facing a problem like this, people will get the film and use it to show the community so they can get some kind of support to fight the problem.

L) But it's a film that is effective not just because of content, but because there's an aesthetic at work. If you had the same content sloppily made or poorly put together, it just wouldn't be as stunning, which is the word that one of my colleagues uses for it. It's visually exciting and structurally sound as well.

M) That's where my interest is—in that end of it—so what I tried to do was unite the two.

L) It worked. Is there anything that I haven't asked you about that you'd like to be in an article or profile of you that you think should be included? I wonder if I'm asking all the right questions.

M) It's so hard when you're starting on the next film. When you're in the middle of production and you're cutting, it's coming to the end. When you start all over again, there's a very insecure state of mind: you've got a blank piece of paper, you've got the armature to put clay on. That's where I am right now. If I'm realistic, it's probably going to take me a year to get a good script and maybe I won't even be funded at that point.

L) You're doing the writing yourself?

M) I think I'm going to try and work with a writer, but I haven't found anyone yet. In terms of the initial story, I'll do it myself and then if I can get some money to develop the script, I'll hire a writer to work with.

L) How do you find a writer?

M) Writing to me is very difficult. When I was first coming out of sculpture, I had trained my mind to work in a three-dimensional kind of way. Switching from that to writing was very difficult for me. Also, working one-to-one, just working with the clay, you're not talking to people, you don't have to sell anything.

L) What about the promotional aspect? Did that come easily to you?

M) The what?

L) The promotion. Having to sell, to do the fund-raising, the business side. It seems as if you were very successful.

M) The fund-raising went smoothly for me. A film really isn't made by one person, it's really a crew of people involved in it. It's all their talents also that make it happen. A good percentage of the film is working with people as well as having an image of what you want and trying to get it. You've really got to be able to work with the people who are working on the film.

L) That's what it means to be a director.

M) And that I found very emotionally draining and very difficult to do.

L) But there is a bottom line, isn't there, when there are certain things that you have, to do yourself, certain decisions that only you can make?

M) Yes, you have to make certain decisions, but if you're going to get the most out of all the people involved, you really have to allow them to move around and feel as if they're giving to the project. It's sometimes difficult, at least it was for me, having had to deal just with myself and a product, to deal with people on an emotional level at the same time that you're trying to think creatively. I found it difficult to switch from fund-raising to working on an aesthetic level, writing the material, editing, to go from writing proposals and talking to funders and thinking in that mode to creatively trying to bring the project to life.

L) It's another aspect. Artists that I know who work in art forms like painting or sculpture find that self-promotion is the hardest part of it. But it's something you cannot turn away from if you're a filmmaker. You can't forego the business side.

M) In fact, you probably can't make films unless you can do it or hire someone to do it for you.

M) Film is very much a business, not just a matter of aesthetics. Regarding mainstream directing in Hollywood, is that something you might ever have as a goal someday down the road when you're 50 or so?

M) I don't know. It just seems so confining and at the same time so appealing in terms of the money available if one were able to break into it. But my feeling is that artistically it would really be confining. When you've got a big budget, and everyone's watching, you can't take any risks.

L) What's the best movie you ever saw?

M) I've seen some great films lately. Have you seen *Yol*? It's a Turkish film, incredible. And there's another, a Hungarian film, *Constant Still.* Some great films out. Usually you see one great film every three or four years, but recently I saw several in a short time. I recently saw another film by Peter Lillienthal, which isn't out yet. It's called *Mr. Wonderful* or *Looking for Mr. Wonderful,* which was very good, too.

L) In terms of mainstream Hollywood type films, are there any that ever inspired you?

M) No, not really. I love *Pixote.* That was such a good film.
I do think there's incredible discrimination. You can add that.

L) Why do you think that?

M) Well, just the obvious. Look at how many men directors there are in comparison to women directors; there's got to be some problem. But I haven't been confronted with it personally or directly. I don't know specifically why, but obviously there's a problem if you can't name the women directors.

L) You can name them. You can say Elaine May . . . and . . . unfortunately, you can probably enumerate them very quickly. There's Amy Heckerling now. [The director of *Fast Times at Ridgemont High.*]

M) She and Bob went to school together.

L) When you were talking about Hollywood, you said how hard it is for women to succeed. You think it must be discrimination because it's not a lack of talent, and, obviously, there's a lot of talent. What about access to the camera?

M) It's hard to break in, for example, as a camerawoman, because usually when you start as a cameraperson you start as a camera assistant, which involves picking up heavy equipment, or being a gaffer. You have to work your way up through the ranks. Many women are not big and strong. You work your way up through a lot of manual labor positions—lifting, carrying. Also, there's a blue-collar old boy network. Why are there so few women? That's why I say there must be discrimination because there'd be more women directing otherwise.

L) How does the discrimination work? Does it work because they're not coming up through that blue-collar network?

M) I don't know. I would assume there's a network in Hollywood that you have to break through, and that's why there are so few camera-women and so few women directors in Hollywood. There's probably an almost invisible network.

L) Even when Lee Grant wanted to make a film, she had to go through a lot.

M) But she's a well-known actress.

L) But she's not getting Hollywood money.

M) Even so, it was probably easier for her than for most women; maybe not, but the fact that she was well known as an actress gave her some access to those people who put the projects together financially. Actually women produced *Tell Me a Riddle*, too; they raised the money. I think there are a lot of women producers.

L) I think there are more women producers than directors in mainstream Hollywood.

M) But I'm sure it was very hard for Claudia Weill, for example. Being a director is a very, very, very tough job, and then you bring all the sexual stereotypes that the crew members and everyone else have and it just makes it that much harder. If you're directing, it's like an army operation; you're the general and you have a hundred troops, most of whom are men; half are grips and electricians and all that. They're not going to want to listen to a woman. They're rather blue-collar sexist guys; every second that you don't get them to do what you want them to do is costing you so many thousands of dollars. It's an extremely tough job. Most men couldn't handle it.

There was an article I read concerning Claudia Weill. She had said that even though she had much more money to do a Hollywood film—*It's My Turn,* the last film that she made—she felt restricted. She didn't have artistic control over the product.

L) That's what everyone negotiates; who will have the final cut, which the studio tries to keep, especially maybe with a woman director.

M) And I guess you don't get it until you're really established.

CHRONOLOGY

Passing thru Linden

Upcoming release

In Our Water

1982

LINDA YELLEN

Photo credit: Fran Grill.

Linda Yellen was born in New York City on July 13, 1950. She still lives in New York and works at Warner Brothers, also in New York City. She has a B.A. from Barnard College (1970); an M.F.A. in film from Columbia University (1972), and a Ph.D. in language, literature and communication from Columbia University (1974).

Yellen is a member of the Executive Council of the Directors Guild of America, The Writer's Guild, and The Academy of Television Arts and Sciences.

Articles written by or about her have been published in *The New York Times; The Village Voice, Interview, Hollywood Reporter,* and *France Soir.*

She is a screenwriter, executive producer, producer and director of many films and videos. To date, her television projects have received thirteen awards, including seven Emmys, two Peabodys, one Luminas, a Silver Nymph, and two Christophers. Her films have been selected to be shown at the Cannes, Monte Carlo, New York, and Deauville film festivals.

Yellen is currently the producer/writer of *Margaret Bourke-White,* a feature film spanning twenty-five years of the life of the noted photographer. The project has been developed for Barbra Streisand to both star in and direct.

Playing for Time, the true-life drama of a death camp orchestra made up of inmates forced to play for their survival.
Photo caption: CBS Television.

Jane Alexander (front, center) stars as Alma Rose, a talented musician imprisoned at Auschwitz who becomes the leader of the concentration camp's orchestra. .
Photo credit: CBS Television.

Vanessa Redgrave gives a powerful performance as Fania Fenelon, survivor of Auschwitz and a member of the death camp's orchestra in *Playing for Time*. Photo credit: CBS Television.

Jane Alexander as Alma, the orchestra's leader in *Playing for Time*. Photo credit: CBS Television.

Vanessa Redgrave as Fania Fenelon in *Playing for Time*. Photo credit: CBS Television.

INTERVIEW

Interview with Linda Yellen, February 13, 1984, in New York City. She is the producer of *Playing for Time* and *Prisoner without a Name, Cell without a Number.*

LM) I had met you briefly at the Barnard reunion.

LY) Yes, but it was a little hectic.

LM) I'm the media librarian at Rutgers University, and I had done work with women artists in the other visual arts before I became the media librarian, just to give you a little background on me and why I'm interested. I came to film and realized that just as women artists have very often not been treated the same way, or supported—if you want to use that word—as men are, so women film and video directors or producers have often been shoved aside. My interest in that area grows. I have done a book of interviews with women artists, on their backgrounds, their lives, their work, of course, and how these elements have interacted. I have a continuing interest in women in the arts. In television it's apparent that the producer is the person who has the final cut. Is that right?

LY) Yes, because directors are brought in for a relatively short period of time and they're invariably not the ones who created the idea. It's the producer who has created the idea or optioned or purchased the book that served as the basis of the idea and worked with the scriptwriter to comple-

237

tion of a script that was acceptable by the network. It's only at that point, when the network says it's acceptable, they're going to put up the money to make the movie, that you bring in a director. So, unlike feature films—where a director often is the creative force brought in even before the writer, when there's just a concept—they come in for, I would guess, a period of four weeks preproduction. Sometimes it's a lot less. I've done several pictures where they've come in for a week or two of preproduction, then generally four weeks of shooting, and about four weeks of postproduction, whereas, if I'm in the role of producer, I can be spending a year or more on that same project.

LM) So it's your project, you're the one who initiates the idea, who hires the director?

LY) Yes.

LM) In television, as opposed to film, the director works only with the actors and you work with the crew?

LY) No, that isn't how it's done.

LM) How does it divide up?

LY) The difference is that in television—I guess this really is a very individual thing—some producers feel a lot less creative than others. I consider myself a very creative producer, and I retain final control of casting and of a crew. I mean, I want to hire a crew that the director's happy with and have the director veto people. By the same token, I will not hire a crew that the director's happy with but I'm not because if it should occur that I'd feel a necessity to fire the director, I'd have to feel that there's a crew that I am comfortable with.

LM) Have you directed?

LY) Yes, for *Prisoner without a Name, Cell without a Number*, I served as producer, director, writer, and that was the last film. Prior to that, what really got me into the television business was that I had produced a low budget feature. Even before that there were the two films at Barnard, the feature on the Columbia riots and the short *Prospera.* It was the first film to come out of Barnard.

LM) What was the title of the low budget feature?

LY) *Come Out, Come Out.* That was the call by the police to the kids to come out of the buildings; it was also such a revolutionary time, come out of yourself.

LM) And a child's game, tag. Have you ever played tag? Hide and seek? Come out, come out, wherever you are?

LY) Exactly. Also, I felt a lot of it was a game, a pose.

LM) Do you think of yourself as an independent producer now?

LY) Well, an independent dependent. Because the budgets of my films are of a certain cost, I can no longer do what I did starting out and be totally independent. I'm independent in the sense that I'm not, at the moment, locked into working with only one network or one studio; I can bring projects to all of them. But I recognize and desire teamwork in combination with a network or studio. I think it's a very desirable way to work.

LM) How does that work? Do you get an idea, then go to a network, and make a contract?

LY) I go to a network with the idea. If they like it, they may say, "We like that idea, we'll develop it with you," which means they'll pay for the screenwriter. If there's an option on the book, they'll pay all or part of the cost of optioning the book. If it's an expensive book, generally, they'll be paying part of it. I'll have to arrange for the other payments.

LM) Then . . . ?

LY) For six months to a year, sometimes longer, I'll work with the screenwriter generally through two drafts and a polish—sometimes more. I will bring in the network at each point where there's a draft to look at to get their comments. Actually, there are several people at the networks who have a kind of creative bonding. It's very, very good. It's very fruitful because sometimes you can be so close to a project that you lose the benefit of an overview from a distance. When they do see it and read it, the network officials that I work with, that I have this relationship with, are often very, very astute in pointing out, gee, if we just change this or we change that. . . . Of course, we try to accommodate that.

LM) That never becomes a problem because they're paying? You've never been uncomfortable with that?

LY) It was only once that I fought them, once,

and in that instance, I simply would not go forward with the project. I'm talking about once out of better than two dozen network projects. I think that's very good odds.

LM) It sounds as if it's not a censorship issue; that [kind of] freedom can be an advantage for an independent but not in-house producer.

LY) There are very few producers working in house.

LM) From the little bit that you just described to me, and from what I have seen here during the few minutes I was waiting for you, I think you're very close to your people, including the director and everyone. You're shaping it at every step, working with the writer and the director. Do you think that this is typical of the industry?

LY I don't think it's typical. I think it exemplifies what can happen as more creative results and teamings occur. For me, it's a necessity because what I really love in filmmaking is the creative process. Unfortunately, all of us in the business today have to spend far too much time dealing with business. Furthermore, because I have a set idea in my mind about which way I want the project to go, if I didn't give that input, I would not get the results I want with even a second, or third, or fourth stab at it. I have a very high success ratio in the industry of projects put into development that are eventually made. There's normally an enormous drop-off level of producers' projects somewhere going awry in script and the project is abandoned. I think if an idea was good enough to interest a network to begin with, good enough to get me enthusiastic about it, then it's still good enough, and, therefore, there must be some way of working and reworking the material that would be true to the original concept that got everybody excited. And I just make that my practice.

LM) You usually work with original material, but with the last project, *Prisoner without a Name, Cell without a Number*, you essentially adapted Timmerman's book, which had been a series of articles in *The New Yorker*. Sometimes it can become controversial with the original author. I'll give you an example; I'm thinking of I. B. Singer and Barbra Streisand and *Yentl.*

LY) I think he's outrageous, absolutely outrageous in his reaction. My admiration and compassion go out to Barbra Streisand, to have completed this heroic job. It is simply untenable that a man like Singer, who has been in the business as long as he has and who signed the contracts, should not have had the business and moral obligation to live up to the contract. Those contracts, I'm sure, stated that Streisand was going to have creative control and final say over the contents and the script and everything like that.

LM) He's had other work adapted for stage and screen.

LY) Yes, he has. He's been around long enough to realize that that is the way things go.

LM) What do you think is going on there?

LY) Well, I think it's sour grapes. I think it's totally in poor taste, really.

LM) Nothing like that has happened to you personally? You haven't had that with Timerman?

LY) No.

LM) He trusted you.

LY) If you remember, Fania Fenelon objected to the casting of Vanessa Redgrave in *Playing for Time.* That was another example where we had negotiated, gave her a very good deal, and there was never any question about her having any approval rights on casting. She was represented by very outstanding agents, who are very familiar with the business. If it is a point of contention with someone, if there's a major point, then they should make that the issue of the negotiations.

LM) The political beliefs of the person playing the part, as opposed to their artistic ability.

LY) No, not that, no, not that. More simply stated it is that if she wanted to have some control over who's playing the part, she should have demanded that as one of the absolute, inviolate points of the contract. That was not the case. What she wanted was more money and that we were able to meet. So, if Mr. Singer, in retrospect, finds it a problem of Miss Streisand's playing the part and is in favor of another actress, who's very good but who could not have gotten the project off the ground and who certainly does not have the talents of a superstar like Miss Streisand, if he had problems with the script and wanted approval of how his work was done, he was represented by very fine agents and should have made those the points of the negotiation. It's simple. In the simplest transaction, it is as if you sell me a suit for $300 and I buy it and put a flower or something like that on it and you come along, a year or two later, and say, "I want $500 for the suit, and I don't want you ever wearing it with a flower."

LM) Do you remember what films or television programs you watched as a very young child? Do you remember your first movie or your first television program?

LY) I can't say which was first. I remember being scolded for writing on the television set while watching Tom Terrific.

LM) That's interactive video, all right.

LY) There was a screen that you sent away for, a plastic screen that could be put on the set. I guess this was in the mid-fifties or something like that, and then you could, your child could, draw along with the images. But I didn't have the screen, and I drew along anyway. I loved the Lucy series and "Amos and Andy." I thought they were marvelous. I don't really remember any serious drama on television. I also loved the feeling of television as it was then; I think it's far less that way now. It was so much of a family event. You know, you turned on Ed Sullivan or put on "The Show of Shows." I don't really remember "Show of Shows," I'm a little too young for that, but I remember the feeling of it. It's been brought back so many times in movies like *My Favorite Year*, I almost feel as if I remember it.

LM) The whole family would gather around, just like a ritual.

LY) It was really great.

LM) You'd go over a friend's house . . . that would just be the center.

LY) Family communication. Of course, now, in modern families, everyone has their own individual television set.

LM) And their own favorite show.

LY) And their own video machines. So they tape it if they missed it. It's changed a little. As for movies, I remember being very moved by *Showboat*, the remake of *Showboat* in the fifties that stayed in my mind. As a kid, I wanted to see *West Side Story* time and time again.

LM) Musicals.

LY) Musicals. I don't know why because I can't sing a note, but I've always had an affinity for musicals. I did love movies. My parents, my mother is, was, is a movie buff. In fact, if we had any historical questions we wanted to ask, about who's in a movie, what year something was made, or what was the plot, when we failed with our resource material, we called my mother.

LM) I love that.

LY) It's true. Really true.

LM) Is she a librarian?

LY) Oh, she well could be—on movies. She used to take me to the movies at least twice a week, from about the time I was two.

LM) Most parents thought it was excessive to go once a week.

LY) I guess there were not a lot of friends.

LM) I guess she was taking you because she wanted to go.

LY) She loved to go, too. Also, I didn't like being with babysitters. I remember being taken to movies like *Butterfield 8* as a child. There were no codes at the time, official rating codes such as we have today, but there were some self-imposed codes and it was considered terrible to take a child of twelve, or even older, to such a movie.

LM) With Taylor and Clift?

LY) Yes, for, in a sense, she was playing a woman with loose morals, and I remember my grandmother taking me to that and people on the line getting into a huge fight: "How dare you take a child to see this kind of movie?" Amazing how values have changed because we see that sort of thing, far more explicitly, on television every day of the week.

LM) At that age were you thinking of becoming a film or television person?

LY) With my background it was all right to look at movies and to go all the time, but it was not the sort of thing anyone was ever expected to do professionally, it was just not. It was a different world. I was going to say it's not the thing a "nice" girl did. I was expected to become a doctor. I even did have a small stint at medical school to try to please my parents; the fall-back position was to become a professor. Either job would just be a prelude, a means of biding my time, before I married well. And then, since I was a very good student, when I did start getting involved with these things, about the time of high school, I always got involved behind the scenes. There would be a production of a play, and I would be the editor of the playbill. There would be a "Sing." I don't know if they have them throughout the country, but at New York schools, various classes compete with each other by putting on musicals. Well, I would head, in a sense I would be the producer of all three "sings," but I was not the person in the forefront, like the editor of the school newspaper. At that point, I thought my affinity for movies would make me become a film critic or a film historian or something like that. Which, in fact, I did.

LM) You wrote about it.

LY) I wrote about it.

LM) Where was this high school?

LY) Forest Hills High School. Home of Simon and Garfunkel.

LM) It seems that your current role as you were describing it to me has a business aspect. Were you ever interested in just going into business?

LY) No, not at all. I do have a good business head, I'm told, but only as it relates to doing this. For that reason, over the last five years, which is really when I've emerged as an established film-maker in the industry, I've always had partnerships. I've always wanted them, and agents, lawyers, and what not, and I've always tried to relegate as much of the business activity as I can to those people to allow myself the most time for the creative aspects.

The Chrysalis Company maintains a midtown office. When business has to be conducted, I'll call there, I'll go to the agent's office. I keep this little work space down here for the creative things, where I'm not encumbered by people coming in, looking for jobs.

LM) It's more like a loft, an artist's studio.

LY) Yes, that's exactly it. I chose a place like this because very often in the creative process we have to walk the floor at night to get a script done. We want to have a nice kitchen here, a home feeling.

LM) I can see it. I have a master's degree in theater; I don't practice, but I have worked on theater productions, and I know what it is to get something going either as director or technical crew member.

So, when you were in high school, you were doing theater work, but behind the scenes; you were writing, but were not thinking of yourself as a filmmaker or television producer.

LY) Right.

LM) So what happened?

LY) I went to Barnard. I'd like to take out an ad, "How Barnard changed my life," because it did. It was wonderful. About the second or third week at Barnard an interesting thing happened. I had gone there, thinking, "Oh well, everybody else will be a lot brighter than I." I looked so young, I had a baby face at that point. I thought I looked so dumb; I wished I needed glasses because a good pair of hornrimmed glasses mature you. At one point, I actually bought a pair with plate glass, or borrowed them, just to have a nice serious look.

LM) What class were you in?

LY) 1970. Even though there were a lot of very, very bright women at Barnard at the time, many of them, even the brightest, did not have the ease that I had in public speaking. It was a requirement to make speeches in all the English classes. These women were terrified, whereas it came relatively easily to me. They simply couldn't do it.

LM) You were an English major?

LY) Yes. One day, they were casting around for two women, girls, to play the two spirits in *Dark of the Moon*. There's a blonde spirit and a brunette spirit, like temptresses or witches. I was sitting next to Susan McKinley, my best friend at Barnard College. We were just like alter egos all through Barnard. I had long blonde hair down to my waist, she had long dark hair. Bert Stimhal, who was then directing at Barnard, came and said, "You two, I want you to audition for this play." Well, it just knocked me out, because I think secretly I'd always wanted to do something like that, but I never would have the courage to go off and do it. We auditioned, and we both got the parts.

LM) It was type casting.

LY) Type casting. It was wonderful, just an event, and I felt very good about doing it, except that sometimes I had reservations when Bert would tell me to do certain things. My instincts told me that it would be better to do something else. I learned then that that's the role of the director, to try to mold the part, and I thought I could do this really well. I think I have more of an affinity for it. I think if I had been directing myself, I would have had better results. So, when the next opportunity came along at Barnard, I said, "What I'd really like to do is direct, if there's something that comes along you think I'd be comfortable with, I'd like to direct it." Kenneth Janes, KJ, whom I adore, had just written a play the summer before when he was at, I think it was, RADA, The Royal Academy of Dramatic Arts or some other very prestigious group. Maybe it was the Bristol Vic, I don't know. He'd written a play on the War of the Roses, during the time he had been writer in residence; it was called *Towton*. It was a perfect play to mount at Barnard, because it was all about the wives of the soldiers whose husbands had gone off to this war. Normally, college plays are dismal for an all girl's school because the girls have to play the boys' parts as well.

LM) You'd have to go recruit somebody from across the street.

LY) So, I directed that play.

LM) Was this in the context of a course?

LY) No, this was all extracurricular. It was put on at Minor Latham Playhouse at Barnard in the winter months. I had worked very hard for what seemed like a long time; it must have been two weeks or so, but then it seemed like a long time. There was a big snowstorm, and very few people came the weekend it was presented. One of the people who did come was an elderly gentleman, who came backstage after the performance to congratulate me. He said I did a marvelous job direct-ing this. He said, "Have you ever thought about directing summer theater?" I think I was sixteen at the time. I said, "I'm not interested in the theater," and he said, "Well, why not?" At that time, there was talk that the New York theater was dead, and I was echoing it; he laughed. He said, "Well, what is it that you'd like to do?" I said, "I'd really like to make a movie." He said, "Why?" And I said, "Well, you know, a movie is something you always have with you. You can take it around to friends' houses and show it to them." Eventually he gave Barnard the money to enable me to make my first movie. He was Richard Rodgers. I was so embarrassed.

LM) Your first patron.

LY) My first patron.

LY) And that movie, of course, was *Prospera,* about a girl who lived in a tree. You hear so much about making a movie, in terms of dealing with networks and studios, that that was far easier than making a movie that would not be offensive to anybody at Barnard.

LM) Would you have had to do that?

LY) Oh, sure. That was implicit, rather than explicit. So we chose a delightful fairy tale about a girl who lived in a tree in Central Park and made that her home.

LM) Was it based on somebody else's story or . . . ?

LY) No, Susan McKinley, Anna Latella, and I, and a few other girls in our Barnard class, sat down and wrote it. The film was very successful and won all sorts of awards. It was shown at the New York Film Festival and honored, at a time when there were two other films that were honored among the shorts. One was *THX 1138*, made by George Lucas; another was *Italian American*, made by Marty Scorcese, and my little film.

LM) Was that his film school film?

LY) I don't know. I didn't know who they were. It was only years later when we were reviewing playbills that they gave out that I realized who these guys were; I didn't know at the time.

LM) How did it feel to have the money and a project and to be doing it at a relatively young age?

LY) It was so thrilling. I loved being challenged. In fact, certainly to this day, and, I hope, in the next thirty, forty years—as long as I'll be lucky enough to be in this business—I'll always find challenges. When you're young and starting out, you know nothing about how a movie is assembled. Everything is a challenge. And that's very exciting.

LM) How did you do it? You had the money and you had the ideas. You didn't have any filmmaking background. Did you just learn through trial and error?

LY) Yes, a lot of trial and error. Also, we used the money to hire a couple of professionals. We had a professional cameraman, and we had a professional editor—not really an editor, because we did the editing—a postproduction man, an elderly gentleman, and we borrowed some space. We also had the innocence, of sixteen- and seventeen-year-old

Barnard girls and a cause. We were outrageous. We went to Joe Levine's office and asked him to give us something for free; he donated editing rooms for us. We went to the city and they gave us all sorts of police help, to help secure the areas. Everywhere we could, basically, we asked for handouts, and got enough to do it, and to compensate for the trial-and-error part of what we were making.

LM) You didn't have any classes?

LY) No, there were no classes.

LM) Either in theater or filmmaking?

LY) No, actually, at that time, I had had a class. I had started taking college classes when I was in high school as part of the Cornell University summer program in sciences. There's this orientation you go to in science. I was an honor student in biology and chemistry. While I was at Cornell I took a three-credit college course in The Art and History of Motion Pictures. Cornell was one of the first places to have it. It was a very hard course.

LM) This was in the 60s?

LY) Yes. I tried to get the credit transferred to Barnard. I spoke to a wonderful lady. She reminded me of Audrey Hepburn if Audrey Hepburn were in her sixties or seventies. She was lovely, she was head of the Art History Department. You see, they didn't know where to send me to get the approval with a course in Art and History of Motion Pictures. Do you send her to the Art Department, the History Department, or the Art History Department? And this wonderful lady said to me, I guess this was in 66 or 67, "My dear, I would no more credit a course in filmmaking than a course in table setting." It was such a wonderful thing that three or four short years later, I was teaching the first course in film at Barnard. I like to think that my activities in film went part of the way to changing these values at Barnard.

LM) Where did you get the cameras for the film?

LY) In the yellow pages.

LM) In other words, you didn't have it. You did not have access to any of those materials in school.

LY) No, no. They didn't exist.

LM) So you had to be entrepreneurial.

LY) It's the best way. When I was teaching film, while going to graduate school, I was really against—I think in some large degree I still am today—teaching filmmaking. I think it's a very artificial thing to teach within the university. People should go out, apprentice themselves to filmmakers—the unions have wonderful programs for that—and intern.

LM) Do you have interns and apprentices?

LY) Oh, yes, definitely. On every film. And what an outlet. Gofors, be a gofor. It's the best way to pick up knowledge. While I was at Barnard, I wrote an article for *The Barnard Bulletin* on Otto Preminger. It was very lauditory and he liked the article very much. He invited me to be young-film-maker-in-residence when they were making *Tell*

Me That You Love Me, Juney Moon. That was a
fantastic experience.

LM) His daughter Eve went to Columbia Law
School.

LY) Yes, I think so. Or his niece, I think it's his
niece.

LM) He has stood up very powerfully on the
issue of artistic control. Is it true that he doesn't like
his films shown on television, or refuses to give
permission?

LY) I don't know.

LM) He doesn't like what happens when the
film is punctuated by commercials.

LY) I don't know, but that's kind of unrealis-
tic in today's world because I think that no matter
how successful your movie is, you reach far more
people through television. The numbers are just
staggering. The economics of movie making are
such today—it's so expensive to make a movie—
that it would be not impossible, but very, very hard
for a movie to go into profit without having those
auxiliary markets like television and syndicated
television.

LM) That's why you chose television rather
than film?

LY) I just fell into television. I was geared,
and I still am, to a motion picture career, though
now that I've been in television and love it the way I
do, I'll always like to continue doing things in television. I've been in television for four or five years

now, and I guess my goal for the next four or five years is to establish myself in the motion picture field as well.

LM) I want to go back to talking about your early experiences. You told me that your mother and grandmother used to take you to the movies. But when you desired to become a filmmaker, after you made *Prospera*, were you encouraged by your parents?

LY) Oh, no. Now my mother forgets—she says, yes, that I was—but it's not true. I wouldn't have gone through as many years of postcollege education, and I wouldn't have gone the route of teaching, and the stab at medical school if I had really been encouraged in this as a career. That's okay. Now, they're really, really thrilled with my success. They're very supportive of my projects, even the difficult ones, even the ones that cause controversy and stress. They're very support-ive. But that's only been in the last three years, I guess.

LM) Were your parents involved with the arts, other than being viewers?

LY) Not at all. I'm the only person in the arts in my whole family.

LM) What about business?

LY) No, no. They're all in the sciences.

LM) That's interesting. You talked about the Art History woman, who was rather discouraging. Were any teachers at Barnard encouraging to you as a filmmaker?

LY) Well, it didn't have an air of reality about it.

LM) Barnard? Or . . .

LY) No, filmmaking. Barnard seemed very real at the time. But, Jean Walsh, do you remember Jean Walsh? One of the deans, of administration, I think. She was marvelous. Also Barbara Novak. Kate Stempson lent us her apartment at one point. We blew a fuse. Her fuse blew during the filming. And Kate Millett. There were a lot of people who were excited by films. They didn't get actively involved. Maristella Lorch is the one who pushed to have me co-teach that course in Italian film.

LM) That was her course.

LY) Yes. What happened was that there had never been a course in film up to that time. She was chair of the Italian Department, and was very encouraging about trying to move Barnard into films slowly. Since I was so enamored of the Italian film directors we devised this together, and I was the instructor.

LM) As an undergraduate?

LY) I think it might have been my senior year, or if it wasn't my senior year, it was my first year in the graduate program.

LM) What did you take in graduate school? Filmmaking?

LY) No, no. Then I knew for sure that film was my area. Remember, I had already done a feature film on the Columbia riots.

LM) You did that when you were in school?

LY) I was an undergraduate, and so I knew what was happening. As a result of Donald Rugoff's seeing that film—he was then president of Cinema 5—Rugoff theaters offered me my first serious job at Cinema 5 as a film buyer and story editor. It was a wonderful job because I'd never been to Europe before. I got to go to Europe at least once a month to look at films, and to recommend what films should be brought back here for distribution. I studied for two years at the Columbia School of the Arts; I got a master's degree in film criticism. After that I got my Ph.D in language, literature and communication.

LM) So you're a doctor.

LY) My parents got their doctor. At that point, I used to threaten to someday list that on the credit of a film—Doctor Yellen—directed by Doctor Linda Yellen, but now it sort of embarrasses me.

LM) You could always become a university faculty member if all else fails.

LY) I do get such a kick and such inspiration from the interns that we have every year that I would love to teach a course. I guest-lecture quite a bit. I enjoy doing that. I actually get something back. It's not just my putting out the ideas, the perceptions, it is also to be attuned to others. Having been out of school for ten years, I am made aware of how much has gone on in that time.

LM) So you stopped teaching formally.

LY) Yes, there's no time.

LM) You talked about Otto Preminger as a

person you looked up to. Did you have any other mentors, or specific role models, people that you would try to be like? Besides Preminger, who gave you a boost?

LY) There is no such thing as making it on your own. I've been very, very fortunate in that along the way there have been so many people who recognized a spark of talent in me, or maybe identified with me in my quest, remembering what they had gone through. All along the way, people have reached out and taught and helped and opened doors. My contention, looking back at Barnard, is that, because I'm a perennial optimist, all you need is a willing ear. If there is a willing ear, someone's listening; then you have a chance to make an impression, make a difference. What I found, which is probably not surprising at all, but it was a little bit then, is that the most established people, the higher-ups, are the ones who are most generous of their time and capable of making things happen, making the connections, and molding situations. I credit people like Bill Feitelson, who is a very famous show business attorney. He saw me when I came to a party; he was very encouraging when I was a student of his. Feitelson used to get a kick out of my desire to be in film and would help me write little contracts on the backs of envelopes, because I couldn't possibly afford to pay the legal fees. Then he introduced me to a bright young man, Jerry Loree, who was not so young but was so in his eyes. He became my lawyer for a number of years, and we're still very good friends. You need a competent lawyer because you do need to be legally protected. I credit Henry Rogers, who served as a mentor; he's president of Rogers and Cowan, a big public relations firm. He was the first to introduce me to people. It is very important to be known. Of course, my agent, Alvin Perlburg. After making my first low-budget feature, *Looking Up*, and people were taking me to lunch, taking me to dinner to talk about being my agent, he was the only one who said, "I'm going to take you to ABC."

LM) That's more important than eating.

LY) That's more important than lunch or dinner and he's been a sort of mentor. Steve Mills and Bill Selk at CBS, Bud Grant, there's oh so many people; the list could just go on.

LM) It's interesting to me that you're telling me about men, and you're not telling me about women.

LY) I'm naming names of those early on. Now, today, the picture is different, within the space of two or three years. It's also the levels of things, too. Today, I credit women like Bridgette Pather, who's a vice-president at HBO, and was at ABC at that time. Bogie Boatwright, who's vice-president at MGM; Diane Sokolow, vice-president at Warner Bros.; Lucy Fisher, another vice-president at Warner Bros. These are the women who are really helping. Nancy Behan, who is a director at CBS.

LM) Are you saying that in the early days, they just weren't there?

LY) Well, we're only talking about a difference of two or three years; they were there, I just didn't meet them. It's just circumstance. They've been there. Remember, also, the big difference is that I was much more firmly based in New York, and wasn't given an opportunity to explore the people in California. Now, I go there regularly. I would have to say that I really don't hold to the theory that the opportunities aren't there for women. What I also want to say is—I don't know if this is what you were leading up to—I don't believe that women are not helpful to women. Again, you find that lower echelon people are often afraid to help someone on the way up. In some strange way, which I've never understood, they somehow feel that somebody else will be above them, and they don't like that.

LM) You think it's more to do with position than gender.

LY) I do, I do.

LM) Did you have any idols? Somebody you always wanted to be exactly like when you grew up?

LY) Everytime I see a movie I really love, the people involved with that movie become my idols for a short time. I don't have one particular idol.

LM) You said you wanted to take an ad in favor of Barnard. You felt that your education, in spite of the fact that there were no classes, was good. That Barnard contributed to your growth as a filmmaker.

LY) Very much so. Again, I started off by saying I don't believe in filmmaking classes. I think, really, the basis of all films should be the written word. When we see wonderful films that are beautiful to look at, they sometimes go off when the story is not right.

LM) A bad text.

LY) A bad text and that's where, I think, I'm lucky to have as strong an English Lit background as I do. I feel that it's not only given me an understanding of language, of story, but a very good understanding of overview. I can realize the whole construct, whereas so many filmmakers my age are so caught up with the visual image of filmmaking that they lack the content underneath it. I have striven in my films such as *Prisoner* or *Playing for Time* or even the lighter films to have such a story to tell.

LM) Let's talk a little about the whole issue of feminism, being a woman in the industry. Has it made a difference? You seem to be saying it made almost a positive difference. Since you were a young girl you got all the help you needed.

LY) I think I would have gotten the help if I had been a young man, too. By the time I came into the industry, many women had already broken ground in the area of producing and writing. I didn't have any problems to speak of because of my sex. The challenge for the 80s is in the area of directing, which is something I love doing in combination with producing or on its own. The role of the director has become very important to a film project. It wasn't always that important in feature films, and now it's the key element along with the stars, the key creative element. The opportunities for women have been few and far between and as happens with any minority, in something like that, if a woman directs a bad movie, it's terrible for every other woman who's trying to direct a movie. If a black goes ahead and commits a crime, all blacks suffer. It's not that much different. Because of that, I feel an enormous obligation when I'm directing that I not only do a good job for myself, but for the other women who are doing it. I believe, based on my conversations with men and women in the industry, that the agonies are over, but we are at the ground-breaking level.

LM) It's almost like "damned if you do, damned if you don't." If you're successful like Streisand with *Yentel*, people are going to attack you because you altered material or make up some excuse, and if you're not fabulously successful they'll attack you because you're not. I feel it's a big dilemma for women directors.

LY) The industry tends to examine big successes like a Streisand and compare them to Spielberg when he did *1941*. They're all waiting for him to fail and, of course, he bounced right back with the next film. Barbra Streisand "failed," but I don't think it's a failure in any terms, really. I think it's a big success. It's the classic story, I think, of a lot of jealousy all around. I don't think she was being damned by it; I think she's having the last laugh. Her picture is not only artistically successful, it's becoming a financial success. She set out to do a very, very hard job, a very hard job, because it was not a conventional film as a money maker or a vehicle for her. She had a lot of strikes against her and she pulled it off. As for lesser successes, there are many numbers of men who've made charming small films and have great difficulty getting to do their next films. I think they do have it a little easier than women, and the reason I think they have it easier is because the women who've made their charming films have tended to make women's films. These have tended to be of subjects and attitudes, and of a style that critics could label "women's films." Everyone says it's very, very valuable when starting out as a filmmaker—just like a writer starting out is supposed to write about what they know the best—for women to choose familiar material. It also is damning, for it just locks them into that genre.

LM) Even though women are a huge percentage of the audience, I don't know what percentage they are . . .

LY) Well, it's still men—teenagers. The biggest audience is the teenage audience and teenage boys ask teenage girls out to the movies and they pay for the tickets and they choose the movie. It doesn't change. My first big directing job was this Timerman movie. I didn't care what people said about it, good or bad, though I hoped good. It did turn out pretty well, but I didn't want it labeled a woman's film. I didn't want that label attached to my first big stab at directing. I turned down some other directorial work because I was so conscious of veering away from it. But no one said George Cukor couldn't direct fabulous women's films like *The Women* because he was *not* a woman. I don't believe the same standards should apply. Indeed, the women who have made really commercially successful films, such as Elaine May, when she did *A New Leaf,* or Lina Wertmueller with *Seven Beauties,* did not make women's films, they just made films.

LM) I'm interested in the Jewish content of your last two major projects, especially in light of the article in *Film Comment* about film and television treatment of Jewish material. Is that something that interests you, presenting Jews in the mass media, or is it just that those are interesting stories and you wanted to tell them?

LY) Growing up, one has to come to terms with a lot of things about oneself; being a woman and being Jewish for me were certainly two. The image of Jews in the world, the way that people who are non-Jews deal with Jews, and mostly the way Jews view Jews are something that is of importance to me. Basically, I believe in the oneness of humanity, when you scrape away everything else, and that's a major point I try to make in *Playing for Time* and again in the Timmerman movie. I am, I think, emotionally drawn to material about Jews and particularly about Jews during the period of the great oppression, which was the Holocaust period, because anyone who's alive today and Jewish must have gotten the idea, "there but for the grace of God, go I." Therefore, there's some responsibility to making sense out of what happened. But many are like the character Fania Fenelon, who considered herself an artist first and a Jew second. And Timmerman considered himself a fighter first and a Jew second. I'm a filmmaker and an American who's proud of my Jewish heritage. I don't really seek out projects; they sort of hit me, they come to me, and say, "Make me; you're going to make me." Something catches my attention, and I just can't get it out of my mind.

LM) What are you working on now?

LY) I'm working on the Brigitte Bardot story, which I see as a very feminist story. I'm delighted to say that although people have tried to sell the Bridget Bardot bio pic or docudrama to all the networks, no one would touch it. And I'm very proud that they never did. It's really wonderful. It just was boring, another bio, they've done so many. There's a whole list. I saw her story as really a feminist issue because one day when I opened a book, *B.B.*, which has since been optioned, to the center, there were pictures of every female star I know of and admire. At one point or another in their careers, the female stars looked like Bardot, modeled themselves on her. Bardot said things about how she wanted to live her life like a man, some have said, with arrogance, some have said to create a kind of mystique about her. But, still the things she said in the 50s, the rest of us didn't even begin to think about until twenty years later.

LM) How old is Bardot now?

LY) Fifty.

LM) Have you met her yet?

LY) No, I've not met her yet.

LM) Does she know about your project?

LY) Yes.

LM) That would be exciting. I hear she's still very beautiful.

LY) We're also doing a success story, a success story like *Rocky*. We're doing *The Second Serve*, the story of Doctor Renee Richards; quite possibly Vanessa Redgrave will be playing both Dr. Richard Raskin and Renee Richards.

LM) That will be exciting. That theme has been fascinating for the last several years. Transsexuality, not just cross-dressing, but true transsexuality. It's been dealt with comedially in *Garp*. It's never really been treated with the respect it deserves.

LY) And then I guess my major project at the moment—there are many others, because you always have to keep a lot of balls in the air—is the true story of the man who is the forefather of the Solidarity movement, a non-Jew, a real hero, a real living hero, a man named Jan Novak. He never wanted to be a hero, never wanted to be a spy, any of those things, and had to turn his whole life around; he became the messenger, took all the secret messages back and forth between the Allies and the Polish base. He was the first man to see Stalin begin to destroy Poland and take it over.

LM) Is he still alive?

LY) After the war, he spent the next thirty-five years of his life as the voice of Radio Free Europe, and he's sentenced to death in exile from Poland, his mother country. He's living in Washington, D.C. He's an advisor to our government in the whole area of communist affairs. He's an expert. And he was the man whom Lech Walesa as a boy listened to night after night. When the Solidarity movement began, they published an underground newspaper. It was one of their first activities; the name of the paper was *The Jan Novak*. It's his story, which is a remarkable story. It reads like the best espionage story. The message of his story, which may really be a message to women in films, is that we may not reap the benefits of a lot of the seeds we sow in trying to make things better for maybe another generation or two. I think that's okay.

LM) So don't be impatient?

LY) Don't be impatient.

LM) You have so many things going on. You said that this last piece that you talked about will be a feature film released in theaters, and you're working in the studios. It's amazing that you can keep all these balls going. Do you have separate production companies working simultaneously?

LY) You generally set up a production company when you actually get to the shooting. Until that time, it's all a lot of files.

LM) I'm very interested, because it seems that either you were a natural humanist who found reaffirmation at Barnard or you learned humanism there or somewhere. It seems that a central focus in most of your work is this humanist theme.

LY) That's interesting. It's interesting because another big influence on me in school was Theo Gaster. I was lucky to be one of the students to take his course. Up to that point I had, I guess, resented my Jewish education because I didn't understand it.

LM) You had had a Jewish education?

LY) Oh, I was even Bat Mitzvahed. I hated it. I can't remember anything except the one phrase which means, "Can I please be excused to leave the room?"

LM) "Can I go to the bathroom?"

LY) No, it was meaningless because it didn't have any context or anything sensible. I remember being thrown out of the Hebrew school class when they were selling sponge cake for Passover. I had raised my hand and said, "I don't understand how if the Jews leaving the desert didn't have enough time to let the bread rise, where they had enough time to make raisin-filled sponge cake." I was thrown out. That was the nature of the education.

LM) Skeptic.

LY) Then I came to Theo Gaster's class, and we were asked to read the great philosophical treatises which became bases for many religions and that is the best example of the oneness—I haven't thought about this for years. You read those treatises, and underneath them all, there are the same goals, the same anxieties. You may or may not know I've been asked to be chair of the Barnard Committee on the Arts.

LM) Oh, that's wonderful.

LY) I'm quite excited about it, too. That's going to be in May.

LM) At the reunion?

LY) No, near the reunion time, but it's going to be separate from the reunion. I really blossomed when I went to Barnard; it was a whole different experience. I was a grub in high school. It was a New York City high school where everybody competes with each other just to get that extra point, to get a 97 average, to get into Barnard. Once I got into Barnard, I found a whole different atmosphere of comraderie, and since then I've tried to live my life away from competition. I'm in competition with myself. I think that is why I still stay in New York. And why the things I choose to do on television are off the beaten path for the most part. There must be a million projects on incest right now at the networks; it's fashionable. I feel there's a place for that, but I don't want to get into it.

LM) The best incest piece I've ever seen is Jean Cocteau's *The Beauty and the Beast.*

LY) Ohhh.

LM) People don't usually think of it in terms of incest. I saw it again the other night. If that isn't an incest story, I don't know what is.

I don't want to take up too much of your time because I know you have other appointments. Is there anything else you'd particularly like to comment on?

LY) I'm sorry, I can't really think of any now, but you're very welcome—I don't know when you need this—to call anytime.

CHRONOLOGY

Hardhat and Legs	1981
Playing for Time	1981
Mayflower: The Pilgrim's Adventure	1980
Looking Up	1978
Come Out, Come Out	1970
Prospera	No date
The Mythmaker	No date
The Tenement	No date